Links

To Your

Canadian Past

Tome 3
Ontario, Manitoba, Saskatchewan, Alberta, British Columbia, Yukon and the Northwest Territories

---

Peter J. Gagné

Quintin Publications
Pawtucket, Rhode Island

ISBN: 1-58211-120-0

Printed in the United States of America

First Edition
First Printing, March 1999

Quintin Publications
28 Felsmere Ave
Pawtucket, Rhode Island 02861-2903
Telephone: 401-723-6797
Fax: 401-726-0327

Website: http://www.quintinpublications.com

Cover: Map of Ontario , H.B. Walker, Montreal, 1910 in the possession of the publisher.

Table of Contents

Publisher's Notes

Thousands, if not millions, of new genealogical websites have appeared during the past several years. At times, it seems to resemble a "Gordian Knot" — too many sites, poorly organized, if organized at all, and no regulation. This present publication, *Links to Your Canadian Past – Ontario and the Western Provinces,* is the 3rd of the QUINTIN'S LINKS SERIES and, will hopefully attempt to remedy that situation. Hundreds of hours have gone into the compilation of each book insuring its accuracy and completeness. We have taken particular care in choosing highly qualified authors to research each volume and hope that it will make your genealogical journey one of great pleasure.

Special Note to Readers: Please inform the publisher immediately of any broken links or additional links that you feel have either been left out or were created after the publication of this book.

Please send all correspondence to:

Quintin Publications, Inc.
28 Felsmere Ave
Pawtucket, RI 02861-2903

or

E-mail: WesternLinks@quintinpublications.com

Author's Notes

Names – All names of places and individuals are transcribed *as found* on each Web site. This includes British, American and First Nations spellings of words found in Web site titles.

Abbreviations – Sometimes abbreviations of the names of organizations are included in the site name or description. The full name should appear elsewhere in the title or description. Abbreviations used for states and provinces are as follows:

AL	Alabama
IH	Idaho
LA	Louisiana
MI	Michigan
NB	New Brunswick
NH	New Hampshire
OH	Ohio
PEI	Prince Edward Island
VT	Vermont
BC	British Columbia
IL	Illinois
MB	Manitoba
MN	Minnesota
NE	Nebraska
NWT	Northwest Territories
ON	Ontario
RI	Rhode Island
WI	Wisconsin
CT	Connecticut
IN	Indiana
ME	Maine
MS	Mississippi
NF	Newfoundland
NY	New York
PA	Pennsylvania
SK	Saskatchewan
YK	Yukon Territory

Searching – The term "searchable" has been used in this book to indicate that a search engine is available for the site or database being described, meaning you type in a keyword and the engine returns a list of results. When this method is not available, you can search an individual Web page yourself with your browser. Just hit `[CTRL]+[F]` at the same time to call up the search box in either Netscape or Internet Explorer.

Mailing Lists – Where possible, I have included a link to a Web page with instructions on subscribing to the list. When this was not available, an e-mail address follows the name of the list. Some lists provide you two methods of subscribing: All means you receive all postings individually. **Digest** means you receive a daily or occasional "digest" of postings. Use the address for the option you want. Send an e-mail with *no subject* and just the given text as the body of the message. If **all** or **digest** are not options, include only the word `subscribe` or the given text in the body of the message.

Don't Understand French? – Many of the sites included in this book are "French only" (indicated after the site name or before the URL for sites with long names). This means that the text on the site is only presented in French.
To get a translation, use the AltaVista Translation site
(http://babelfish.altavista.digital.com/cgi-bin/translate?).
You can enter the URL for the Web page you want translated or type in a given section of text, and after a brief pause the translator will return the translation.

Submit a Site – Have you come across a site that isn't included in this book? Do you have a site of your own that you'd like included?
Send an e-mail to Quebeclinks@quintinpublications.com.
Be sure to include the province, category (and subcategory) and URL (Web address) for the site.

Introduction

This book is the result of hundreds of hours of online research. It is meant to serve as a sort of "yellow pages" for your genealogy and history research in Ontario and the western provinces and territories of Canada.

This book is meant to **save you time and confusion** in your online research. By organizing the information geographically, then by resource type, I have attempted to provide you the shortest route to find what you are looking for on the Internet. The Web can often seem overwhelming, and it's easy to get lost or caught in it and feel more like the fly than the spider.

Sure, there are many "lists" out there on the Internet, but none of them provide the **organization** and the **descriptions** that you will find in this book. Many lists just point you to another list, then another and take you to a site three or four clicks from what you are actually looking for – and good luck finding your way back to where you started. Others claim to link you to a specific site, but merely point the way and force you to find it in the context of a larger Web site. Still others merely give you a list of names with no description, and you waste time chasing down links that don't help you at all or miss sites that could provide valuable information for your research.

I have **personally visited every site** listed in this book and written the accompanying description, so you know that when you type in the URL, you'll be taken exactly where you want to go. In the case of pages contained within frames where all of the frame choices are not relevant to the topic, I have linked to just the individual frame that is appropriate.

This book in on paper and not on the Internet for one main reason: it can't be deleted, erased or "crash." Keep it by your computer and use it to **decide where you want to go before you go online**. That way, you'll save time surfing, reduce connection time and make your online time more efficient. If you find sites that you want to visit again, "bookmark" them or add them to your browser's "favorites." But in case you lose them, accidentally delete them or your computer crashes, this book will still be there. and if you use the Internet at your public library or another location where you don't have your own set of favorite sites, take this book along.

Good luck in your research, and happy surfing!

-Peter J. Gagné

Internet/Computer Glossary

Terms in Italics refer to other glossary entries.

Bookmarks: A collection of your favorite sites (on Netscape Navigator). Bookmarks are basically a collection of links to sites that you visit often or want to go back to, without having to re-type the entire *URL* over and over. *See also Favorites.*

Bps: Bits Per Second. This is a measure of how fast data is transferred through your modem. "K" stands for thousand, thus 56k means 56,000 bits per second transferred.

Browser: The computer program that you use to view Web pages, images and other documents and files on the *Internet.* The two most popular browsers are Microsoft Internet Explorer and Netscape Navigator. (Netscape Communicator is a "browser suite" that integrates an e-mail program, *html* editor and other features.)

Cache: A reserved area of your hard drive or memory where files are stored temporarily for quick retrieval. Many Web pages or image files are stored in your computer's cache so they can be accessed quicker than downloading them off the Web each time.

Cookie: A piece of information stored on your computer that is used to identify you to Web sites. Some sites use cookies as a means of keeping track of your identity and password, so you don't have to type in a username and password every time you visit. Other sites keep track of your preferences or customized user options for activities on the site. Some sites may use cookies to try to find out information about you without your knowledge. You can set your browser to accept or reject all cookies or warn you before accepting cookies.

Discussion List: Also known as "mailing lists." A discussion list is a list of people who decide to send and receive e-mail messages pertaining to a certain subject or topic. List members join the list by "subscribing," and then send messages to the group by "posting" a message to the list. Some lists offer the option of subscribing to every message posted to the list or to just a daily or occasional digest of postings. "Moderated" lists are run by an individual who screens posted messages.

Domain: In the *URL* `http://www.YourName.com`, "YourName" is the domain. The domain is the identifier for groups or individuals on the Web.

FAQ: Frequently Asked Questions. Many sites provide them to reduce the amount of actual questions that they get posed through e-mail.

Favorites: A collection of your favorite sites (on Microsoft Internet Explorer). Favorites are basically a collection of links to sites that you visit often or want to go back to, without having to re-type the entire *URL* over and over. *See also Bookmarks.*

FTP: File Transfer Protocol. This is a way of sending files from one computer to another, and is most often used to download files from the Web or send files from an individual's computer to a Web *server* to be posted on the *Internet.*

GIF: Graphic Interchange Format, pronounced "giff." A type of image file used in Web pages. GIF files are usually drawings or computer-generated images. Some GIF files are "animated" and appear to move or change shape.

Host: A company or group that provides storage space on their *servers* for Web sites.

HTML: HyperText Markup Language. This is the language used to write Web pages.

HTTP: HyperText Transfer Protocol. This is the set of rules that computers use to allow you to view HyperText documents, or Web pages.

Hyper Link: Part of a Web page or *HyperText* document that allows the user direct access to another Web page or document.

HyperText: A type of computer file that allows the integration of text, images and other multimedia elements into a single file, usually a Web page. HyperText also allows the linking of one file to others through hyper links.

Internet: Commonly confused or interchanged with the *World Wide Web.* The Internet is the combination of the Web, e-mail, *ftp* and other means of exchanging data.

Interstitals: Small *browser* windows that pop up and display advertisements or other information. Interstitals are most common in *online communities*, where the *host* provides free Web space in exchange for displaying advertisements.

ISP: Internet Service Provider. These are the people that you pay to get on the Web. They provide the connection between your computer and the *Internet.* Some of the bigger national ISPs are AT&T WorldNet, MSN, EarthLink and MindSpring.

Java: A programming language used in Web pages to run mini-programs or "applets" on Web pages. Some of the more common examples of the use of Java are news tickers, changing images, chat rooms and buttons that change color or reveal another image or information when the pointer passes over them.

JPEG/JPG: Pronounced "J-peg." An acronym for Joint Photographic Experts Group, an industry collective that agreed on the standard for this type of image file, most often a scanned photo.

Online Community: A group of Web sites bound together by common themes and interests. Online communities commonly provide free Web sites to individuals or groups in exchange for displaying advertisements on these sites or in *interstitals*. Some of the more popular online communities are GeoCities, Tripod and Xoom.

Online Service: An ISP that provides its members with pre-packaged content or "channels." These channels are on the online service's *servers*, and while online services provide access to the *Internet* at large, they are not the Internet itself, but are more like a closed community or "Disney World" version of the Internet. Some of the more popular online services are America Online, Compuserve and Prodigy.

Plug-ins: Small programs that extend the capabilities of your *browser* to view different types of image, music or other files.

Protocol: A set of rules that computers use to communicate with each other. *See FTP, http* and *TCP/IP*.

Search Engine: A Web site that searches the *Internet* to find the site or keyword you are looking for. Many search engines don't search the entire Web, but rather the sites that have registered with them or which they have indexed. Some of the more popular search engines are Yahoo!, Excite, AltaVista, Lycos and HotBot. A search engine that searches other search engines is known as a meta search engine. Examples of meta search engines are Dogpile and MetaFind.

Server: A computer that stores files that are used by several other computers, known as "clients." A Web server stores the *HTML* and other files that make up Web pages.

Spam: Unwanted, unsolicited bulk e-mail, usually offering some sort of promotion.

TCP/IP: Transmission Control Protocol/Internet Protocol. TCP handles how computers send and receive information between each other. IP breaks up the information being sent into "packets" and assigns each a sequence order. The packets are then sent along different channels to their final destination and put back together in sequence.

URL: Uniform Resource Locator. Commonly called a "Web address." This is the line you type in (which usually begins with `http://`) to get to the site you want.

World Wide Web: Commonly confused with the *Internet*, of which it is a part. The World Wide Web is a network of computers connected via phone lines, and is thus a "dial-up network." The Web is the part of the Internet that stores and displays *HTML* documents and other files on Web sites.

National

Genealogical, Historical and Cultural Societies

Individual Societies

Alliance for Canada's Audio-Visual Heritage [English & French]
http://www.rcc.ryerson.ca/Alliance/
Preserves and facilitates access to heritage materials that include film, video, television and radio productions and sound recordings. Also conducts training programs and aids research projects.

Asian Canadian
http://www.asian.ca/
Dedicated to tracing and sharing the legacy of Asians in the fields of the economy, culture and politics in Canada. Links to professional and media groups, educational and cultural centers.

Association for Canadian Jewish Studies
http://fcis.oise.utoronto.ca/~acjs/
Formerly the Canadian Jewish Historical Society, the ACJS encourages scholarly research in Canadian Jewish history, life and culture. The Web site features news and events, a discussion list and links to research organizations, as well as the *Canadian Jewish News* Internet edition.

Canada GenWeb Project [English & French]
http://www.geocities.com/Heartland/6625/cngenweb.html
A collection of links to genealogical information and data for the entire country. Links to individual provinces' GenWeb sites (catalogued below), with county-level divisions.

Canada's National History Society [English & French]
http://www.cyberspc.mb.ca/~otmw/cnhs/cnhs.html
Dedicated to popularizing Canadian history through an admissions discount program, historical booklet publications, a heritage award and *The Beaver* magazine, with an online index.

Canadian Association for Irish Studies
http://www.usask.ca/english/cais/index.html
Fostering and encouraging the study of Irish culture in Canada. CAIS publishes a semi-annual newsletter (available online) and the twice yearly *Journal of Canadian Irish Studies.*

Canadian Aviation Historical Society
http://www.cahs.com/
Supports and encourages the preservation of Canada's flying heritage through research and collection of historical material. Publishes a quarterly journal. Several provincial chapters.

Canadian Committee on Labour History
http://www.mun.ca/cclh/
Promoting and publishing scholarly research in the field of Canadian labour history and related areas. Books for purchase and an index to the latest newsletter *Labour/Le Travail* available.

Canadian Doukhobor Society
http://www.kootenay.net/~cds/
Information on membership, events, workshops, publications and an online newsletter.

Canadian Friends Historical Association
http://home.interhop.net/~aschrauwe/
Preserving and documenting the social, cultural and pioneer heritage of the Quakers who immigrated to Canada, from their early settlement through today.

Links to Your Canadian Past

Ontario and the Western Provinces

Canadian Heritage / Patrimoine Canadien [English & French]
http://www.pch.gc.ca/
The official page of the Ministry of Canadian Heritage, with the sections: The Department, Multiculturalism, Sport, Canadian Studies and Youth, Canadian Symbols, Human Rights, Cultural Development, Arts and Heritage, Parks Canada and Official Languages.

Canadian Heritage Information Network (CHIN):
http://www.chin.gc.ca/e_main_menu.html
Réseau Canadien d'Information sur le Patrimoine (RCIP):
http://www.rcip.gc.ca/f_main_menu.html
A directory of Canadian museums, galleries and heritage information. Subscribe to special resources, enroll in a course, purchase publications, view virtual exhibits and more.

Canadian Historical Association / Société Historique du Canada [English & French]
http://www.yorku.ca/research/cha/
The CHA advocates the study and preservation of Canadian history by lobbying governments, holding conferences and publishing a journal, historical booklet series and the *CHA Bulletin.*

Canadian Jewish Historical Society
http://www.oise.on.ca/webstuff/otherprj/cjhs1.html
Sponsors an academic journal, a members-only newsletter and an online discussion group.

Canadian Oral History Association / Société Canadienne d'Histoire Orale [English & French]
http://www.ualberta.ca/~fmillar/coha.htm
COHA helps individuals plan and carry out oral history projects. Includes guides and advice.

Canadian Railroad Historical Association – St-Constant, QC
[English & French]
http://www.exporail.org/
Dedicated to the preservation and dissemination of information, artifacts and archival materials pertaining to the history of railways in Canada. The association operates a museum/archives (*see National / Museums and Historic Sites*) and publishes a bimonthly magazine and newsletter.

Canadian Society of Mayflower Descendants
http://www.mayflower.org/canada/canada.html
The society is open to any person able to document his or her lineage to a passenger on the *Mayflower*. Includes research tips and a list of *Mayflower* passengers who left descendants.

Genealogical Institute of the Maritimes
http://www.shelburne.nscc.ns.ca/nsgna/gim/index.html
This organization, focusing on Nova Scotia, Prince Edward Island, Newfoundland and New Brunswick, certifies and registers researchers as either Genealogical Record Searcher (Canada) or Certified Genealogist (Canada). Certification guides available.

Icelandic National League of North America
http://users.imag.net/~sry.rasgeirs/default.html
Seeks to promote the Icelandic language, literature and culture among those of Icelandic descent in Canada and the US.

International Internet Genealogical Society – online resource
[English, French, etc.]
http://www.iigs.org/index.htm.en
This online "society" seeks to link genealogists and genealogical information throughout the world and also provides a chat room, monthly newsletter, queries and free online courses.

Mennonite Historical Societies Directory
http://www.goshen.edu/mcarchives/directory1998.htm
A contact list for North American Mennonite, Amish and related historical committees, societies, conference historians and interpretation centers.

Organization for the History of Canada
http://www.acs.ucalgary.ca/~osnhc/
Dedicated to fostering an interest in the "Canadian national experience" in the broadest sense. OHC publishes *National History*, a quarterly journal devoted to scholarly research and general interest in history, culture, biography, politics, geography, society, and economy.

Pier 21 Society
http://pier21.ns.ca/
A group dedicated to preserving and documenting the history of immigration to Canada through the historic Pier 21 in Nova Scotia and other entry points. Online newsletter and stories.

Ukrainian Genealogical and Historical Society of Canada
http://www.feefhs.org/ca/frgughsc.html
Basic information on the society, contact information and a link to the Ukrainian Research List.

Professional Organization

Federation of Canadian Genealogical and Family History Societies
http://www.rcip.gc.ca/f_main_menu.html
An umbrella organization for societies nationwide. Co-ordinates the exchange of information between societies. Members share current issues, concerns and information on heritage projects.

Links to Your Canadian Past
Ontario and the Western Provinces

Archives

Directories

Canadian Council of Archives Directory of Archival Repositories
http://www.cdncouncilarchives.ca/dir.html
This site provides a comprehensive directory of member institutions and their collections. Archive centers are listed by province as well as theme or type (military, religious, native organizations, etc.).

Canadian Archival Resources on the Internet
http://www.usask.ca/archives/menu.html
This site, maintained by the University of Saskatchewan archives, provides a Web directory of archive centers, listed alphabetically, by region or type.

Archive Centers

Canadian Institute for Historical Microreproductions
http://www.nlc-bnc.ca/cihm/cihm.htm
The CIHM locates early printed Canadian materials, puts them on microfilm and makes them available to libraries and institutions. Includes a list of libraries with a complete or partial collection of the Early Canadiana research project, plus a searchable database of the project, with the possibility to order materials located via the search.

Canadian Pacific Railway Archives
http://www.cpr.ca/www/insidecpr/aboutcpr/cparchives/incprarchives.html
This private archive offers fee-based research services on its materials relating to the history of Canadian Pacific, including the railway, ships, hotels, promotion of immigration and tourism, etc. Images of sample documents, artwork and artifacts are available online.

Canadian Quaker Archives at Pickering College – Newmarket, ON
http://home.interhop.net/~aschrauwe/Archives.html
Information on available resources at the archives for researching Quaker genealogy and history.

Canadian Women's Movement Archives – Ottawa, ON
[English & French]
http://www.uottawa.ca/library/cwma.html
Located at the University of Ottawa, this archive center preserves the documents and archival material of the various women's organizations that collectively make up the women's movement in Canada. This site describes the various holdings and available finding aids.

Charles Denny Métis Genealogical Collection
http://www.glenbow.org/archhtm/denney.htm
This Web site lists the families included in the Denney collection of Métis genealogies housed at the Glenbow Archives in Alberta, giving the call numbers of the microfilmed files. The families included have some connection to the Red River settlement.

George Back Collection from the National Archives [English & French]
http://www.schoolnet.ca/collections/back/
An online presentation of several paintings, maps, documents and artifacts from Back's Arctic expeditions pertaining to Alberta, Manitoba, the Northwest Territories, Ontario, Saskatchewan, the Yukon Territories and the sea.

Hudson's Bay Company Archives
http://www.gov.mb.ca/chc/archives/hbca/index.html
Information on the holdings of the HBCA, how and where to access records, a catalogue of microfilm holdings, and a list of libraries and repositories. The site also includes a brief history of the Company and online aids to help locate and order available records.

Métis Genealogical Research Services – Glenbow Archives
http://www.glenbow.org/archhtm/metis.htm
Contains information on the Métis genealogy research service of the Glenbow Archives in Alberta, including fees, contact information and records searched.

National Archives of Canada [English & French]
http://www.archives.ca/
Includes a comprehensive guide to using the archives and a Genealogy Research section with information on census, birth, marriage, death, land and many other records in the archives' holdings. There is also a page on How to Get Started and information on how to make inquiries.

United Church of Canada/Victoria University Archives
http://vicu.utoronto.ca/archives/archives.htm
Describes the holdings of the United Church of Canada and its antecedent denominations, including the Presbyterian and Methodist Churches in Canada. Also includes information on genealogical research and resources at the archives.

Professional Organizations

Alliance of Libraries Archives and Records Management (ALARM) [English & French]
http://www.fis.utoronto.ca/groups/ALARM/
A forum for those working in the various fields of information management, ALARM provides a Marketplace/Directory listing of educational and training resources in the field, plus an Open Forum/Personal Interaction area, where professionals can communicate and interact.

Association of Canadian Archivists
http://www.archives.ca/aca/
A group providing government advocacy, leadership, communication and awareness of archival concerns and issues in the professional community. Publishes a newsletter and scholarly journal.

Association of Canadian Map Libraries and Archives [English & French]
http://nexus.sscl.uwo.ca/assoc/acml/acmla.html
A group of map librarians, cartographic archivists and other interested in preserving geographic information. Promotes professional standards, research and publications. The ACMLA also offers maps of Canadian cities for sale on its Web site, with thumbnail previews.

Canadian Council of Archives [English & French]
http://www.cdncouncilarchives.ca/
The national coordinating body for federal and provincial archives groups. Their bulletin is available online, as is a list of publications and information about the Canadian Archival Information Network initiative to put archival information online.

Records Management Institute
HTTP://www.dfait-maeci.gc.ca/rmi-igd/menu.htm
A professional organization dedicated to the needs of those in the field of managing recorded information. The RMI promotes sound standards and practices, encourages and facilitates the exchange of information, organizes and promotes conferences and training. This site provides information on all their activities, links to articles, a mailing list and newsgroup.

Libraries and Research Centers

Directories and Catalogues

Canadian Libraries and Library Catalogues [English & French]
http://www.nlc-bnc.ca/canlib/eindex.htm
A searchable listing of libraries throughout Canada by province, name or type. Some libraries just provide information, while others allow a search of their catalogue.

Canadian Library Index
http://www.lights.com/canlib/
A listing, by province, of the Web sites of libraries throughout Canada. Each listing contains a link to the library's Web site and/or their telnet or Web-based catalogue.

Family History Centers in Canada
- http://www.shelburne.nscc.ns.ca/nsgna/fhc/cdnfhc.htm
- http://www.genhomepage.com/FHC/Canada.html

Lists (the first by province) of the addresses and phone numbers of LDS Family History Centers.

HYTELNET Library Catalogues: Canada
http://moondog.usask.ca/hytelnet/ca0/ca000.html
A listing of the TELNET sites, login names and procedures to search online catalogues of public and university libraries throughout Canada.

resAnet [English & French]
http://www.amicus.nlc-bnc.ca/resanet/
The catalogue of the National Library of Canada. resAnet is a free subset of the fee-based Amicus catalogue, providing brief records of the library's collections.

Special Collections in Canadian Libraries [English & French]
http://library.usask.ca/spcol/index.html
An index to the contents of special collections of libraries throughout Canada. Browse through subjects such as History, Cartographic Materials and Sociology or search for a specific keyword.

WebCATS – Canada
http://library.usask.ca/hywebcat/countries/CA.html
A listing of links to Web-based catalogues of public and university libraries across Canada.

Libraries and Research Centers

Canadian City Directory Collection – National Library of Canada

- http://library.usask.ca/spcol/collections/040e.html
- http://www.nlc-bnc.ca/services/edirect.htm

A description of this specialized collection – over 7,000 volumes of directories from across the country at different levels, with access and holdings information.

Links to Your Canadian Past

Ontario and the Western Provinces

Gabriel Dumont Institute of Native Studies and Applied Research – Regina, SK
http://schoolnet2.carleton.ca/english/ext/aboriginal/metis-de/dumont.html
Promoting the renewal and development of Métis culture through research and education.

National Library of Canada [English & French]
http://www.nlc-bnc.ca/ehome.htm
Information on the collections and services of the National Library, which include access to its electronic collections and a description of Services to Genealogists and Family Historians. These services include the fee-based catalogue Access AMICUS and a listing of reference sources for Canadian genealogy.

Royal Military College of Canada: Massey Library
http://library.usask.ca/spcol/institutions/32e.html
Describes the Canadian Military History Collection and the Reginald E. Watters Collection at the library, with contact information for the library.

Canadian Studies Centers and Programs

Acadia University: Canadian Studies Program (Wolfville, NS)
http://ace.acadiau.ca/arts/canstud.htm

Association of Canadian Studies [English & French]
http://www.er.uqam.ca/nobel/c1015/e_acs.htm
The only national association dedicated solely to the promotion of research, teaching and publications on Canada. The ACS sponsors conferences, publications, awards and study programs at the college and university level, as well as other educational levels.

Links to Your Canadian Past
Ontario and the Western Provinces

Association for Canadian Studies in the United States
(Washington, DC)
http://canada-acsus.plattsburgh.edu/acsus/i_acsus.htm
The only organization in the U.S. devoted to encouraging and supporting the study of Canada's political system, economy, history, geography, literature and artistic and cultural heritage. The ACUS sponsors conferences, grants and awards as well as various publications in the field, including a newsletter, *Canadian Studies Update*, available online.

Association Françaises d'Études Canadiennes/French Association for Canadian Studies
http://www.archimedia.fr/AFEC/index.html
A multidisciplinary association promoting Canadian studies in France through scholarships, a scholarly journal, conferences and communication among France's Canadian studies centers.

Athabasca University: B.A. Major in Canadian Studies
(Athabasca, AB)
http://www.athabascau.ca/html/programs/b_arts/maj_cdst.htm
A description of the program and listing of sample courses in literature, geography, history, native and ethnic studies, politics and government.

Canadian Studies in the United States (online resource)
- **Main**: http://canada-acsus.plattsburgh.edu/index.htm
- **List of Programs**: http://Canada-acsus.plattsburgh.edu/programs/orgprog.htm

A joint project of the Center for the Study of Canada at SUNY Plattsburgh and the Association for the Study of Canada in the U.S., this site is an online resource center for material pertaining to Canadian Studies. Sections include Business, Conferences, Government, Grants, Newspapers, Outreach, Positions, Programs and Video, as well as recent news items.

Links to Your Canadian Past
Ontario and the Western Provinces

Capilano College Canadian Studies Specialty (North Vancouver, BC)
http://www.capcollege.bc.ca/programs/cana_studies/index.html
A listing of courses offered in the specialty and overview of requirements.

Carleton University: School of Canadian Studies (Ottawa, ON)
http://temagami.carleton.ca/fass/CanStud/index.html
Information on the undergraduate and graduate programs, academic staff, faculty research interests, awards and bursaries, recent publications and the school's history and mission.

Center for the Study of Canada – SUNY Plattsburgh (Plattsburgh, NY)
http://canada-acsus.plattsburgh.edu/cesca/cesca.htm
A presentation of the programs of study offered at this institution, including major and minor programs, internships, study abroad, scholarships and grants and other activities.

Centre d'Études Amérindiennes [French only] (Chicoutimi, QC)
http://www.uqac.uquebec.ca/cea/cea.htm
The programs under the auspices of the CEA include a Certificate of Teaching in Amerindian Communities, Certificate in Native Technolinguistics, Certificate of Multidisciplinary Studies, a Bachelors Degree in Preschool and Primary Education and a Short Caseworker Program.

Centre d'Études Canadiennes, Université de Rennes (Rennes, France) [French only]
http://www.uhb.fr/langues/cec/
A multidisciplinary program focusing on research and teaching of all aspects of Canadian studies. The center organizes conferences, academic exchanges and publications.

Dalhousie University Canadian Studies Programme (Halifax, NS)
http://WWW.Registrar.Dal.Ca/calendar/ugrad/cana/
An overview of the requirements, faculty and courses included in the programme.

Institute of Canadian Studies – University of Ottawa [English & French]
http://www.uottawa.ca/academic/arts/cdn/
Offers undergraduate and Ph.D. programs, workshops, lecture series and seminars.

International Council of Canadian Studies
http://WWW.ICCS-CIEC.CA/eng_home.html
A group of 20 national and multi-national Canadian Studies associations, dedicated to promoting and supporting research, education and publications in the field of Canadian Studies.

McGill Institute for the Study of Canada (Montréal, QC) [English & French]
http://www.arts.mcgill.ca/programs/misc/
The institute offers interdisciplinary and experimental courses in Canadian studies, provides graduate fellowships and hosts visiting students and seminar speakers. It offers both major and minor concentration programs in Canadian Studies and a minor in Canadian Ethnic Studies.

Mount Allison University Programme of Canadian Studies (Sackville, NB)
http://aci.mta.ca/depts/canadian_studies/
Both undergraduate programs and courses for non full-time students are offered, with a particular focus on Maritime history. Course and faculty listing available online.

Mount Saint Vincent University Canadian Studies Program (Halifax, NS)
http://www.msvu.ca/calendar/cana.htm
An interdisciplinary Bachelor of Arts if offered with either a major or minor in Canadian Studies.

Saint François-Xavier University Canadian Studies Program (Antigosh, NS)
http://xel.stfx.ca/academic/Canadian-Studies/
An overview of various aspects of the program, including faculty, courses and students.

Saint Mary's University Department of Atlantic Canada Studies (Halifax, NS)
http://www.stmarys.ca/academic/arts/atlantic.htm
Course descriptions, offerings and time table, as well as faculty information.

Simon Fraser University Centre for Canadian Studies (Burnaby, BC)
http://www.sfu.ca/cns/
General information on the program, as well as faculty, courses and student groups.

Trent University (Peterborough, ON)

- **Canadian Studies Program**: http://www.trentu.ca/admin/ro/calendar/dynamic/canstudies.html
- **Summer Explorations in Canadian Culture**: http://ivory.trentu.ca/www/canstudies/summer.htm

University of Alberta: Undergraduate Programs in Canadian Studies (Edmonton, AB)
http://www.ualberta.ca/~polisci/canstud/ugrad.htm
Offers courses in Canadian regions, culture, literature, nationalism and contemporary issues.

Links to Your Canadian Past

Ontario and the Western Provinces

University of British Columbia: Canadian Studies Program (Vancouver, BC)
http://www.arts.ubc.ca/canada/cdnstud.htm
An overview of the program, with major, minor and specialized course lists.

University of Calgary: Canadian Studies (Calgary, AB)
http://www.ucalgary.ca/pubs/calendar/current/What/Fac/GN/BBMP/DOP/CNST.htm
Details of the requirements for the program and the courses offered in various disciplines.

University of Manitoba Canadian Studies Program (Winnipeg, MB)
http://www.umanitoba.ca/faculties/arts/deans_office/cdnsp.htm
An overview of the program, including courses in Canadian history, economics, politics, and social and cultural traditions.

University of Prince Edward Island Canadian Studies Program (Charlottetown, PEI)
http://www.upei.ca/~regoff/canst_1.html
Requirements for a major or minor in Canadian Studies, with list of courses and faculty.

University of Regina Canadian Plains Studies Program (Regina, SK)
http://www.uregina.ca/printsrv/artscan.html
An overview of this graduate program to study the unique aspects of Canadian Plains life.

University of Toronto (University College) Canadian Studies Program
http://www.library.utoronto.ca/www/uc/can.htm

University of Victoria: Diploma and Certificate Programs in Canadian Studies for International Students
http://www.uvcs.uvic.ca/artsci/cs/
Admissions and application info, curriculum and courses covered in the programs.

University of Waterloo Canadian Studies (Waterloo, ON)
http://www.adm.uwaterloo.ca:80/infoucal/9596/INTER/can_studies.html
Information on the three-year Canadian Studies major, general and honours option programs, Canadian Studies minor, non-major degree and courses offered in the programs.

Birth, Marriage, Death, Census and Other Data Online

Vital Statistics and Parish Records

Canadian and Other Vital Statistics Offices
http://www.gov.ab.ca/ma/reg/vs/sa.htm
Contact information and an overview of fees for provincial Vital Statistics offices.

Records of Births, Marriages and Deaths at the National Archives
http://www.archives.ca/www/svcs/english/BMDRecords.html
An overview of the records contained in the National Archives classified into church records, marriage indexes, civil registration (birth, marriage and death by province) and marriage bonds.

Census Information

Census of Canada: History
http://142.206.72.128/cgi-bin/folioisa.dll/Focus-e1.nfo/query=*/doc/{t2}/pageitems={body}/hit_headings/words=4?
An overview of the need for a census of Canada, past censuses and an historical timeline.

Census Records in Canada [English & French]
http://www.archives.ca/www/svcs/english/GenealogicalSources.html#Census Records
An overview from the National Archives on what records are available, what they contain and where to find them for use in your research.

Information Collected by Canadian Censuses
http://www.virtuel.qc.ca/simmons/CENSINFO.HTM
A list of the categories of information collected in the 1825, 1831, 1842, 1851, 1861, 1871, 1881, 1891 and 1901 censuses of Canada.

Métis Census Indexes
http://www.televar.com/~gmorin/census.htm
Census information from 1827 to 1917 that includes Métis settlers in present-day Manitoba and parts of the United States (North Dakota, Minnesota and Montana).

National Registration File of 1940
http://www.geocities.com/Heartland/9332/natreg.htm
Information on this census-like registration, which is not as restrictive as other records, including what information is provided for men and women and how to obtain copies of the records.

1901 Census of Canada Information
http://www.tbaytel.net/bmartin/census.htm
An explanation of the column headings for this census, with a listing of National Archives of Canada and LDS film numbers for each district and subdistrict, listed by province.

Passenger Lists/Immigration Data

Early Maritime Disasters and Accidents Involving Immigrants to Canada
http://www.cadvision.com/traces/imigrate/disastr1.html
Includes the names of those passengers saved and lost in the disasters.

Emigration from Iceland to North America
http://nyherji.is/~halfdan/westward/vestur.htm
Articles and information on many aspects of Icelandic immigration to the US and Canada, including Icelandic Names, Settlers, Photos and the "Evergrowing Tree" of surnames.

Immigrants to Canada in the 19th Century
http://www.ist.uwaterloo.ca/~marj/genealogy/thevoyage.html
A wealth of information on immigration for this time period. Ship information, passenger lists, immigrant handbooks, information on specific cultural and national groups, etc.

Immigration Records at the National Archives
http://www.archives.ca/www/svcs/english/ImmigrationRecords.ht
ml
Includes information on available records for passenger lists prior to 1865 and from 1865-1935, border entry records 1908-1935, post-1935 immigration records, immigration from China and Home Children.

inGeneas Passenger and Immigration List Database
http://www.inGeneas.com/ingeneas/index.html
A searchable database of passenger and immigration information from the 18th, 19th and early 20th centuries. Returns age of individual, year and type of record found. For a fee, inGeneas will research further information and provide a more detailed account of the record.

Irish Emigrants
http://www.genealogy.org/~ajmorris/ireland/ireemg.htm
A series of passenger lists for ships leaving Great Britain or Ireland in the late 1800's.

Miscellaneous Immigration Index (National Archives of Canada/inGeneas)
http://www.inGeneas.com/free/index.html
Fully-searchable index of various immigration records from the NAC. Clicking on a returned name provides a complete record and clicking on "source" returns full source information.

Naturalization (Citizenship) Records at the National Archives
http://www.archives.ca/www/svcs/english/GenealogicalSources.html#Citizenship Records
Describes what records are available and where to write for detailed information.

Pier 21: The Ships of Pier 21
http://pier21.ns.ca/ships.html
A list of ships that arrived at Pier 21 carrying War Brides, Troops, Evacuees, Immigrants, Refugees, Displaced Persons and other groups. Links to info on some ships.

Profiles: Immigration Research Series
http://cicnet.ci.gc.ca/english/pub/index.html#reference
A series of reports on (recent) immigrants from several countries, describing settlement patterns, family status, education, demographics, income and other details.

Young Immigrants to Canada
http://www.ist.uwaterloo.ca/~marj/genealogy/homeadd.html
A collection of information on juvenile immigrants to Canada. Includes information on Roman Catholic organizations and other denominations, societies and organizations, reformatories and schools, groups for women and non-British immigrants.

Land Records

Land Records – Genealogical Sources in Canada [English & French]
http://www.archives.ca/www/svcs/english/LandRecords.html
Describes the archival materials available through the National Archives, including:

- **Index to Upper Canada Records**: http://www.archives.ca/www/svcs/english/INDEXRG1_E.html #Upper Canada
- **Index to Lower Canada Records**: http://www.archives.ca/www/svcs/english/INDEXRG1_E.html #Lower Canada

Also provides information on provincial land records holdings.

Métis Land Claims
http://www.archives.ca/www/svcs/english/LandRecords.html#Métis land claims
Brief information on the records in the National Archives pertaining to Métis land claims and how to locate this information in the archives or obtain copies.

Adoption Information and Groups

Adopt: Assistance, Information, Support
http://www.adopting.org/
Sections include Especially for Adoptees, Especially for Birth Parents, Free Search Registry, a Chat room, Support Forums and a great deal of other information.

Adoptee Searcher's Handbook
http://www.login.net/inverc/search.htm
An online resource, created especially for Canadians, on Web sites, registries, records, archives, libraries, government and provincial departments and other sources of adoption information.

Adoptees Internet Mailing List
http://www.webreflection.com/aiml/
A forum for the discussion of search and reunion issues. Includes a chat room.

Adoption Information for Canadians
http://www.toddlersonline.com/adopt/
Primarily for those currently seeking to adopt children, this site provides information on agencies, newsletters, support groups, a book list and message board.

CANADopt
http://nebula.on.ca/canadopt/
Adoption information for each province and Canada-wide, including a national registry.

Canadian Adoptee Information Center and Reunion Registry
http://www.geocities.com/Heartland/Plains/1742/
An online registry for adoptees and birth parents searching for each other. Includes lists of adoptees searching, birth parents searching and an online form for sending data.

Canadian Adoptees Registry, Inc.
http://www.bconnex.net/~rickm/
A free service detailing what records are available and how to obtain them, plus a national registry of adoptees/foster children or parents or those seeking to find them.

Links to Your Canadian Past
Ontario and the Western Provinces

Forget Me Not Family Society
http://www.portal.ca/~adoption/
Includes a Canadian adoption FAQ and Resources, Online Support Lists and Newsletter.

Parent Finders of Canada
http://www.ltinc.net/reunion/
This site includes adoption news and issues from across Canada, an adoption reunion registry form, online group support lists and links to other online resources.

Seekers of the Lost
http://www.seeklost.com/
A free international adoption search registry, with over 42,000 people registered.

The Triad Society for Truth in Adoption in Canada
http://www.sfn.saskatoon.sk.ca/community/triad/index.html
Dedicated to reuniting families separated by adoption. Triad volunteers provide service, support groups, peer counseling and conferences and also maintain a national registry.

Legal and Other Data

Wills and Estate Records
http://www.archives.ca/www/svcs/english/WillsEstates.html
A list from the National Archives of provincial sources of probate records.

Museums/Historic Sites/Groups

Directories

Artefacts Canada [English & French]
http://www.chin.gc.ca/Artefacts/e_artefacts_canada.html
Formerly National Inventories, this is an online catalogue of information on millions of museum objects, natural history specimens and archaeological sites throughout Canada.

Guide to Canadian Museums and Galleries (Canadian Heritage Information Network)
http://www.chin.gc.ca/Museums/ [English & French]
A searchable guide to the museums of Canada by name, collection or location. Information on hours, services, collections and activities, with links to Web sites of member institutions.

Heritage Directory (Canadian Heritage Information Network) [English & French]
http://www.chin.gc.ca/Museums/CHER/e_hp_cher.html
A searchable directory of over 450 private organizations and government departments and agencies engaged in heritage activities and conservation. Contact information and scope and type of activities are included in the listings.

History Lands – Canada's Heritage Sites
http://www.interlog.com/~parks/historyhome.html
An overview of this series on History Television, with links to individual episode summaries on various heritage sites throughout Canada, from Alberta's Head-Smashed-In Buffalo Jump to Québec's Grosse Île Immigrant Station, Victoria's Chinatown, and many more.

Images of Parks Canada [English & French]
http://parkscanada.pch.gc.ca/schoolnet/pcimages/homepage/homepage.htm
View photos from national historical sites and parks throughout Canada.

Parks Canada [English & French]
http://www.parkscanada.pch.gc.ca/
The government authority over Canadian National Heritage parks and sites. Individual sites are indexed in the *Museums and Historic Sites* section of each province.

SchoolNet Digital Collections [English & French]
http://www.SchoolNet.ca/collections/E/index.htm
This site provides access to many online presentations in the areas of History, Geography, First Peoples, Social Studies, Women, Government, Fine Arts, Business and Labour.

Ship Information Database (Canadian Heritage) [English & French]
http://susan.chin.gc.ca:8013/basisdbdocs/title1e.html
Search or browse databases containing information on vessels, masters, owners, builders and voyages for ships of Canadian registry or that sailed in Canadian waters.

Museums and Historic Sites

African Canadian Heritage Tour – Amherstburg, Buxton, Chatham, Dresden & Sandwich, ON
[English & French]:
http://www.ciaccess.com/~jdnewby/heritage/african.htm
Five connected heritage sites depicting the communities settled and developed largely by former slaves who escaped to Canada via the Underground Railroad.

Agriculture Museum – Ottawa, ON [English & French]
http://www.nmstc.ca/ag/index.htm
Showcasing Canada's agricultural heritage through exhibits and the only working farm in a national capital. Visit animal barns for the sights, sounds and smells of Canadian agriculture.

Alexander Mackenzie Voyageur Route Home Page – several provinces
http://www.amvr.org/
Stretching more than 10,000 km from Québec City to British Columbia, this route marks the first documented crossing of continental North America by a European. Find online information about the route, the man and the Alexander Mackenzie Voyageur Route Association.

Canadian Canoe Museum – Peterborough, ON
http://www.canoemuseum.net/
Boasting the "largest collection of canoes and kayaks in the world," the museum features birchbark, dugout and modern canoes and artifacts of the canoeing lifestyle.

Canadian Center for Architecture – Montréal, QC [English & French]
http://cca.qc.ca/contents.html
The CCA is a museum and study center devoted to the art of architecture and the related domains of urban planning and landscape design. While its scope is international, the Center features many local and national exhibits, activities and programs and includes an extensive library.

Canadian Military Heritage Museum – Brantford, ON
http://www.bfree.on.ca/comdir/musgal/cmhm/
Exhibits and artifacts recounting Canada's involvement in military deployments from the Seven Year's War to the Boer War, World Wars I & II, Korea and UN peacekeeping missions.

Canadian Museum of Civilization – Hull, QC [English & French]
http://www.civilization.ca/cmc/cmceng/welcmeng.html
In addition to information on location, hours and events, you can also visit the Virtual Museum, browse some of the permanent and temporary exhibits on the history of Canada and find out about research activities at the museum.

Canadian Museum of Flight – Langley, BC
http://www.canadianflight.org/
This site provides information about the museum and its 23 planes on display, as well as the history of aviation in Canada, aviation artwork and a special section for kids.

Canadian Museum of Rail Travel – Cranbrook, BC
http://www.crowsnest.bc.ca/cmrt/index.html
Restored railway buildings (station, freight shed and water tower) and a large collection of restored railway cars and artifacts depicting the history of rail travel in Canada.

Canadian Postal Museum – Hull, QC [English & French]
http://www.civilization.ca/cpm.html
The only museum in Canada dedicated to preserving and interpreting the material heritage of postal communications as an integral part of modern society and communications.

Canadian Railway Museum and Archives – Delson/St-Constant, QC [English & French]
http://www.exporail.org/musee/musee_CRM.htm
Historic train cars, streetcars, railway equipment and structures help tell the history of rail transportation in Canada and how this history is intimately linked to the history of the country itself.

Canadian War Museum – Hull, QC [English & French]
http://www.civilization.ca/cwm/cwmeng/cwmeng.html
Dedicated to the remembrance of Canada's military history from colonial through modern times. Information about the museum's exhibits and collections and a virtual tour of the galleries.

Canadian Warplane Heritage Museum – Mount Hope, ON
http://www.warplane.com/
Take a virtual tour of the museum, with 35 aircraft from World War II to the Jet Age, and a library/archives with books, photos and artifacts on warplane history.

Currency Museum of the Bank of Canada – Ottawa, ON
- **Information**: http://www.bank-banque-canada.ca/english/museum.htm
- **Collections:** http://www.schoolnet.ca/collections/bank/english/index.htm

The Information page gives location and activities information on the museum, while the Collections page presents some of the items from the museum's exhibits, which tell the history of currency, giving special emphasis to the history of coins and paper money in Canada.

Hudson's Bay Company Digital Collections – online [English & French]
http://www.schoolnet.ca/collections/hbc/
Part of the Manitoba Museum of Man and Nature, the HBC Digital Collection is a virtual exhibit of the former collections of the fur trading company. Includes documents, clothing, tools and more from native and Métis cultures, the fur trade and explorations.

Japanese Canadian National Museum and Archives Society – Vancouver, BC [English & Japanese]
http://www.multinova.com/jcnmas/index.htm
Information on this society, created to present and interpret Japanese Canadian history and culture from the 1870's to the present. The site contains historic images, membership and society information and a timeline of Japanese-Canadian history.

Maritime Command Museum – Halifax, NS
http://www.marlant.hlfx.dnd.ca/museum/
Features exhibits, artifacts, photographs and historical documents from the Royal Canadian Navy, in the residence of the commander-in-chief of the British North American Station.

Museum of the Fur Trade – Chadron, NE (USA)
http://www.furtrade.org/
Dedicated to the history of the North American fur trade, including artifacts from British, French and American trappers and companies, as well as American Indian and Spanish traders from the colonial period to the 20th century.

Museum of the Mountain Man – Pinedale, WY (USA)
http://www.pinedaleonline.com/MMMuseum/
Exhibits and a research library presenting the history of the western fur trade, located in the hub of the historic Rocky Mountain Rendezvous system. Includes exhibits and living history demonstrations on the fur trade, exploration and early settlement of the West.

National Aviation Museum – Ottawa, ON [English & French]
http://www.nmstc.ca/nam/index.htm
Museum information, as well as hundreds of images and lots of information on aircraft, upcoming exhibits and the history of aviation in Canada.

National War Memorial – Ottawa, ON
http://www.vac-acc.gc.ca/Memorials/Nationalmem.htm
A tribute to Canada's war heroes, with online photos and text about the memorial.

North American Black Historical Museum and Cultural Centre – Amherstburg, ON
http://www.city.windsor.on.ca/cvb/Northamericanbl.htm
Contains a research library with genealogical and historical materials, as well as African-Canadian exhibits, audiovisual presentations, workshops and conferences.

Royal Canadian Air Force Memorial Museum – Astra, ON
http://aeroweb.brooklyn.cuny.edu/museums/ont/rcafmm.html
Unofficial information and photographs about the RCAF museum and exhibits.

RCMP Centennial Museum – Regina, SK [English & French]
http://www.trakkerinc.com/rcmp/rcmphome.htm
Historical material and artifacts recounting the colorful history of the RCMP, North-West Mounted Police and Canada's western pioneer heritage.

Veterans Affairs Canada: Memorials
http://www.vac-acc.gc.ca/Memorials/memorials.htm
Links to memorial sites abroad commemorating the service of Canadians in foreign wars.

"We Will Remember": War Monuments in Canada
http://www.stemnet.nf.ca/monuments/
An attempt to preserve the history of the hundreds of war monuments throughout Canada in digital form to be accessible on the Internet. Searchable by province.

Professional Organizations

Canadian Conservation Institute [English & French]
http://www.pch.gc.ca/cci-icc/index~1.htm
CCI's mandate is "To promote the proper care and preservation of Canada's moveable cultural property, and to advance the practice, science, and technology of conservation." To this end, they carry out and assist in research, training, funding and advocacy for conservation.

Canadian Museums Association [English & French]
http://www.museums.ca/
The professional group for the field since 1947.

ICOMOS Canada
http://www.icomos.org/canada/
The Canadian National Committee of the International Committee on Monuments and Sites. The site features news and events, mailing lists, papers, articles and publications.

Military, Native and Historic Groups

Military and Mounted Police

Black Watch (Royal Highland Regiment) of Canada
http://www.odyssee.net/~kerra/bwhome.html
Includes a history of the regiment, the Black Watch Association and Battle Honours.

Books of Remembrance
http://schoolnet2.carleton.ca/books/books.htm
Search for the name of a soldier who died in the following six books of remembrance: Newfoundland, South Africa/Nile, Merchant Navy, Korean War, WWI and WWII.

Canada's Air Force: History and Heritage
http://www.achq.dnd.ca/history.htm
Links to numerous articles, photos and memories of over 75 years of history.

Canadian Army Regiments – Index of Web Sites
http://www.du.edu/~tomills/military/america/cargxref.htm
A list – organized by number of unit and also by name of unit – of Canadian army regiments, with links (where available) to regimental Web sites and a description of the content to be found on the site.

Canadian Casualties in the Boer War
http://www.islandnet.com/~duke/boercas.htm
A list of servicemen who died in the conflict, with name and rank, date and cause of death.

Canadian Expeditionary Force
http://www.archives.ca/db/cef/index.html
This site contains an index to the personnel files of the over 600,000 Canadians who were part of the CEF during World War I. It also contains access to the attestation papers of over 100,000 recruits and a listing of the veterans and casualties from Renfrew, Ontario.

Canadian Military Genealogical FAQ
http://www.ott.igs.net/~donpark/canmilfaq.htm
Provides information on what sources are available and how to contact them.

The Canadian Military Heritage Project
http://www.rootsweb.com/~canmil/1837/battles/battleind.htm
Contains information and resources on all aspects of Canadian military involvement, from the French and Indian Wars to World War II, including the Rebellion of 1837, Fenian raids, Red River Rebellion and North West Rebellion.

Canadian Navy of Yesterday and Today
http://www.uss-salem.org/navhist/canada/
A presentation of the ships and aircraft of the navy from World War I to today.

Canadian POW/MIA Information Centre
http://www.ipsystems.com/powmia/
A good deal of information by and about Canadian POWs and MIAs.

Canadian Vietnam Casualties
http://www.ipsystems.com/powmia/names/names.html
A list of those who lost their lives in the war, with links to extended information on some individuals included in the list.

Canadians Who Served in the Maine State Militia in the Civil War
http://www.geocities.com/Heartland/6625/canmaine.txt
A list of individuals, with full name and company and regiment in which they served.

Commonwealth War Graves Commission
http://www.thecommonwealth.org/links/wargrave.html
Dedicated to maintaining the graves of soldiers who died in defense of the British Commonwealth during the two World Wars.

Honour Roll – Canadian UN Peacekeepers
http://www.islandnet.com/~duke/roll.htm
A list of those "who lost their lives in the service of peace."

Millennia Legacy Project (The Maple Leaf Project)
http://orcn.ahs.uwo.ca/legacy/index1.html
An attempt to put together a collection of photographs of each of the over 110,000 Canadian war graves in 74 countries throughout the world into a sort of virtual National War Cemetery.

Military Records Sources in Canada
http://www.archives.ca/www/svcs/english/GenealogicalSources.html#Military Records
An overview of what records are available through the National Archives for the pre-World War I period and from World War I to the present.

Montcalm Passenger List 1936
http://mypage.direct.ca/d/dobee/pilgrim.html
A list of veterans and descendants aboard the *Montcalm*, which sailed for Antwerp and London on the "Vimy and Battlefields Pilgrimage" in remembrance of the Canadian army's role in WWI.

Reenactment Units in Canada
http://www.geocities.com/Yosemite/2069/anglais.html
A list from the Museum of Applied Military History of contact information and descriptions of military reenactment groups in Canada. Links to Web pages of individual units, where available.

Royal Canadian Air Force Personnel – Honours and Awards
- **1939-1949**: http://www.achq.dnd.ca/awards/index.htm
- **1947-1970**: http://www.achq.dnd.ca/postwar/index.htm

Both sites offer an alphabetical index to RCAF personnel who received awards or citations for service, with links to text describing the honor(s).

Royal Canadian Legion
http://www.legion.ca/
Canada's largest veterans and community service organization. Links to provincial branches.

Royal Canadian Mounted Police (Facts on Canada) [English & French]
http://www.infocan.gc.ca/facts/rcmp-e.html
This site, presented by InfoCan, presents the history of the RCMP, broken down into Origins, Transitions and The RCMP Today.

Royal Canadian Mounted Police: Historical Highlights
http://www.rcmp-grc.gc.ca/html/history.htm
An overview of the major events and development of the RCMP from the 1870's to the 1990's.

Royal Canadian Mounted Police: Official History
http://www.trakkerinc.com/rcmp/english/history/histind.htm
The history of the RCMP from The New Frontier, Rebellion and the Iron Road, through Gold Diggers and War, National Growth to the Information Age.

Royal Canadian Mounted Police: A Brief History
http://www.district.north-van.bc.ca/home/history.html
An overview of the RCMP from a 1991 brochure by the RCMP Public Affairs Directorate.

Unofficial History of the Royal Canadian Navy
http://www.geocities.com/Pentagon/6650/rcn00000.htm
A private citizen's view of the men, women and equipment of the RCN.

World War I Canadian Infantry and Cavalry Index
http://www.bookkeeping.com/rings/genealogy/ww1.html
Lists the unit number, original commanding officer, date of sailing, strength on sailing and headquarters on mobilization.
Under construction.

Native and Métis Groups

Assembly of First Nations [English & French]
http://www.afn.ca/
Formerly the National Indian Brotherhood, the AFN is an association of the leaders of First Nations groups throughout Canada. The AFN seeks to devise common strategies on issues of common concern and promote communication and exchanges between nations.

Canadian Métis Coalition – Moncton, NB
http://www.geocities.com/CapitolHill/Senate/7498/
Created to respond to and serve the national or individual political concerns of Métis living in Canada, regardless of their membership or lack thereof in local or provincial organizations.

Centre d'Études Amérindiennes – Chicoutimi, QC
See Canadian Studies Centers and Programs.

Métis Families
http://www.televar.com/~gmorin/
Information on Métis censuses, marriages, families, stories, etc., presented by Gail Morin.

The Other Métis
http://www.cyberus.ca/~mfdunn/metis/index.html
A comprehensive information source, mainly dealing with Métis and aboriginal peoples who are not represented by the larger Métis organizations of the Prairie Provinces.

Tribes and Bands of the United States and Canada
http://www.hanksville.org/sand/contacts/tribal/US.html
A geographical interface to lists of contact information and (where available) links to Web sites of tribal and native groups throughout the United States and Canada.

Loyalists

Loyalist Sources in the National Archives
http://www.archives.ca/www/svcs/english/GenealogicalSources.html#Loyalist Sources
An overview of what records are available concerning Loyalists and where to find them.

United Empire Loyalists Association of Canada
http://www.npiec.on.ca/~uela/uela1.htm
Sections include What is a Loyalist?, the Loyalist Gazette, Membership, Branches, Important Loyalist Dates, Reading & References and Loyalist Links.

1791: United Empire Loyalists
http://www.magi.com/~westdunn/1791UniL.html
A brief overview of the Loyalist movement and how it affected Canada at this time.

Orangeism and Oddfellows

Canadian Orangeism – An Historical Retrospect
http://members.tripod.com/~Roughian/
This site covers many aspects of Orangeism in Canada, including Orangeism and the Military, Trade Unionism, articles on several historic Orangemen, Military and Historic Documents and several stories and images of historical events and places associated with Canadian Orangeism.

The Grand Orange Lodge of Canada – Willowdale, ON
http://www.orange.ca/
This homepage of the Orange Association of Canada includes sections on Orangeism, What is the Loyal Orange Association?, History, Qualifications, links to Provincial Grand Lodges and information on *The Sentinel*, the official bi-monthly publication of the Association.

International Order of Odd Fellows – Family History Research
http://norm28.hsc.usc.edu/IOOF/FamilyResearch.html
Details what info is and isn't available from the group, with a link to local lodge addresses throughout Canada and how to request information.

Orangeism – The Canadian Scene
http://members.tripod.com/~firstlight_2/cdnscene.htm
A brief history of the Orange Association in Canada, with contact information.

National and Regional History and Historic Photos

Exploration and Settlement

Alexander Mackenzie: "A Map of America between Latitudes 40 and 70 North, and Longitudes 45 and 180 West, Exhibiting Mackenzie's Track."
http://www.lib.virginia.edu/exhibits/lewis_clark/ch4-27.html
A map from Mackenzie's book *Voyages from Montreal, on the River St. Laurence, through the Continent of North America to the Frozen and Pacific Oceans; In the Years 1789 and 1793*, with explanatory text on the explorer and his voyages.

European Explorations of America
http://www.vmnf.civilization.ca/reper/r-ch1-en.htm
A presentation from the Virtual Museum of New France on the various European explorers who visited North America between 1492 and 1620. Presented in the form of a timeline.

Henry Hudson: The Life and Times of Henry Hudson, 17th Century Explorer
http://www.georgian.net/rally/hudson/
A great deal of information on Hudson, his explorations and family.

Hypertext Guide to the Exploration of the Canadian Arctic
http://home.navisoft.com/ekkhs/chronlgy.htm
Includes a chronology of events from 1,000 BC to 1819 as well as biographical notes and contributions of individuals from Eric the Red to William Edward Parry.

Northwest Passage: The Quest for an Arctic Route to the East
http://www.nlc-bnc.ca/north/nor-ii/franklin/fran051e.htm
A chronology of exploration from John Cabot in 1497 to R. Hammond in 1989.

Pier 21 Stories
http://pier21.ns.ca/stories.html
Stories submitted by immigrants who arrived through Pier 21 in Halifax or their descendants. Divided into Immigrants, Guest Children, Refugees, War Brides, World War II and Volunteers.

A Scattering of Seeds: The Creation of Canada
http://seeds.history.ca/~seeds/
A Web companion to the 13-part series of documentaries on the immigration of various cultural groups to Canada. Documents French, Ukrainian, Irish as well as recent Chinese, Japanese, Sikh and other immigrants with historical text, photos and even online video clips from the series.

Sir John Franklin: His Life and Afterlife
http://home.navisoft.com/ekkhs/frank1.htm
A lengthy article on the life and career of the famous explorer and his legacy.

Sir John Franklin
- **Naval Career**:
  http://boulder.earthnet.net/~ambranch/hist01.html
- **First Overland Expedition**:
  http://boulder.earthnet.net/~ambranch/artic.html
- **Second Overland Expedition**:
  http://boulder.earthnet.net/~ambranch/hist02.html
- **Final Expedition**:
  http://boulder.earthnet.net/~ambranch/hist03.html

The Vikings: They Got Here First, But Why Didn't They Stay?
http://www.nlc-bnc.ca/north/nor-i/thule/thu-020e.htm
A presentation by the National Library of Canada on the Viking Discovery of North America.

General and Social History

1791: Canada Act
http://www.magi.com/~westdunn/1791CanA.html
A brief overview of the need for and effects of the Canada Act.

Canada Facts and Trivia
http://www.geocities.com/Heartland/6625/cgwfacts.html
Geographical, historical and personal tidbits, anecdotes and superlatives.

Canadian Economic History
http://web.arts.ubc.ca/cliocan/Clionet.html
A server dedicated to maintaining and exchanging information on the economic history of Canada. Includes conferences, notice boards, data banks, information sources, etc.

CanPix Gallery: Great Canadian Image Base
http://www.nelson.com/nelson/school/discovery/images/ncddimag.htm
Over 3,500 audiovisual resources for Canadian studies, including prominent people, events and places; images of Canadian culture; provincial symbols; as well as audio and text files.

Early Canadiana Online / Notre Mémoire en Ligne [English & French]
http://nlc-bnc.ca/cihm/ecol/
A project to scan primary source historical material from the first European contact to the end of the 19th century, focusing on literature, women's history, native studies and the history of French Canada. To include a searchable database of titles in the collection.

Facts on Canada
http://www.infocan.gc.ca/facts/canadagen-e.html [English & French]
A quick overview of many aspects of Canadian history and society, including geographical, political, social and cultural information presented by InfoCan.

Facts on Canada: History [English & French]
http://www.infocan.gc.ca/facts/history-e.html
Sections of this brief overview of Canadian history include First Colonial Outposts, A Country is Born, Westward Expansion, A Nation Matures and A New Federation in the Making.

Heritage Post Interactive [English & French]
http://heritage.excite.sfu.ca/hpost.html
"The Web's first interactive Canadian history magazine."

Index to Federal Royal Commissions [English and French]
http://www.nlc-bnc.ca/ifrc/index.htm
An author or keyword search of the over 150 commissions since confederation. Documentation includes commission reports, briefs, evidence and other resources.

Inter.Canada: Canadian History Documents [English & French]
http://www.naccess.com/~inter.canada/docptr.htm
A vast amount of historical and political documents and accords relating to Canada.

The Walk to Canada: Tracing the Underground Railroad
http://www.npca.org/walk.html
One historian's tracing of a possible Underground Railroad route from Montgomery County, Maryland to Amherstburg, Ontario, using only the methods available to escaping slaves.

Timelines and "This Week/Day in History"

A **Brief Historical Timeline of Canada**
http://www.geocities.com/Heartland/6625/cgwhistory.html
Historical highlights from 1000 to 1982 AD.

The Great Canadian Timeline
http://www3.sk.sympatico.ca/vavrr/time-l~1.htm
A timeline of events that occurred on Canadian soil from prehistory to 1995.

Important Moments in Canadian History
http://www.arts.ouc.bc.ca/fiar/his_home.html
An historical timeline of notable events, broken down into Prehistory to 1800, 1800-1867, 1867-1918, 1918-1945, 1946-67, 1968-present.

Parks Canada – This Week in History
http://parkscanada.pch.gc.ca/scripts/dbml.exe?Template=/thisweek/thisweeke.htm
Historical vignettes that occurred in the current week at Canadian Historic sites.

This Week in Western Canadian History
http://www.glenbow.ab.ca/libhtm/thisweek.htm
Historical highlights and events from the Canadian West for the current week. Previous weeks can also be viewed or searched for specific content.

Sympatico News Express: On This Day
http://www1.sympatico.ca/cgi-bin/on_this_day
Find out what historic events occurred in Canada (or by Canadians) on this day in history.

Confederation

Canadian Confederation: Historical Documents
http://www.nlc-bnc.ca/confed/historic.htm
A collection of documents dealing with confederation, presented by the National Library of Canada, including the British North America Act and 1871 Treaty of Washington.

Canadian Confederation – The National Library of Canada
http://www.nlc-bnc.ca/confed/e-1867.htm
Several subjects dealing with confederation that show the influence of the American Civil War on confederation. Contains the full text of historic documents, a timeline, bibliography and other confederation subjects.

The Road to Confederation
http://www.canoe.ca/InDepthUnity/confederation.html
An article from the Canadian Global Almanac on the issues and events leading to confederation.

Military History

The Canadian Great War Homepage
http://www.rootsweb.com/~ww1can/
Sections include a Timeline, Soldier's Biographies, Women in the War, Famous Canadians, Life of the Home Front, Victoria's Cross Winners and sections on the Army, Navy and Air Force.

Courage Remembered: The World Wars Through Canadian Eyes [English, some French]
http://www.schoolnet.ca/collections/courage/splash.html
A presentation of the role of Canadian soldiers in World Wars I and II, based on personal memoirs, photography, the work of Canadian war artists and the documented exploits of Canadian George Cross and Victoria Cross recipients.

The Valour and the Horror: Canada at War
http://www.valourandhorror.com/home.htm
Based on the TV series of the same name, consisting of three two-hour films depicting World War II campaigns: A Savage Christmas – Hong Kong 1941, Death By Moonlight – Bomber Campaign and In Desperate Battle – Normandy 1944. Includes a forum where visitors can post and respond to messages in a bulletin board format.

Valour Remembered: Canada and the First World War
http://www.vac-acc.gc.ca/historical/firstwar/vrww1.htm
An informative look at Canada's role in the Great War from its entrance into the conflict through Canadian participation in various battles and campaigns to the final outcome and memorials.

War of 1812
http://fingon.norlink.net/~jkeigher/1812.html
A fairly detailed introduction to the causes, development and conflicts of the war.

War of 1812 Web Site
http://www3.sympatico.ca/dis.general/1812.htm
This site presents a good deal of information on the war, including articles on army life, battles, regiments, and other aspects of the war; a chart of British regiments in North America; book reviews; sound clips of fife & drum music and information on reenactments and replicas.

Professional Groups/Commercial History

A Brief History of Canadian Lighthouses
http://members.aol.com/stiffcrust/pharos/index.html
From the 18th through the 20th centuries, with photos. Also includes a bibliography, museums and societies, postcards, stamps and artwork, plus a list of lighthouses in the movies.

The Bank of Canada: Its History [English & French]
http://www.bank-banque-canada.ca/english/histor.htm
A look at the historical debate for the creation of a central bank in Canada, the founding and development of the Bank of Canada and a link to the Bank of Canada Act.

Building Canada [English & French]
http://blackader.library.mcgill.ca/cac/bland/building/index.html
A selection of images from the John Bland Collection of Canadian Architecture – a set of digitized images that formed part of Prof. Bland's class on the History of Canadian Architecture.

Canadian National Railway – Corporate Profile
http://www.cn.ca/cn/english/about/corporate/history/
Read "The CN Story" from Canada's first railroad through privatization of CN, browse a Timeline of events in CN History or look through the Historical Photo Library.

Canadian National Railways Historic Photo Collection
[English & French]
http://www.schoolnet.ca/collections/cnphoto/cnphoto.html
Photos of over 100 years of locomotives, passenger and freight trains, as well as structures and operations of the Canadian Northern, Grand Trunk Railway, Grand Trunk Pacific, Intercolonial Railway, Canadian National Railway and "CN Today."

Canadian Pacific Railway: Feature Articles
http://www.cpr.ca/www/insidecpr/aboutcpr/cparchives/featurearticles/articles.html
Includes the "Steel Wheels" series by Jonathan Hanna on various CPR apparatus and Heritage Columns by Dave Jones on aspects of CPR history.

Cultivating Canadian Gardens: The History of Gardening in Canada [English & French]
http://www.nlc-bnc.ca/events/garden/eintro.htm
This site, presented by the National Library of Canada, takes an in-depth look at the "leisure activity" of gardening in Canada through the books, periodicals and printed materials in the collections of the NLC from the agricultural activities of the Hurons until our time.

Education in Canada (Facts on Canada/InfoCan) [English & French]
http://www.infocan.gc.ca/facts/educ-e.html
An overview of the educational system in Canada, including a look at the provincial responsibilities, the broad federal role and the various levels of education.

High Flyers: Canadian Women in Aviation [English & French]
See Canadian Women's History.

History of the Canadian Red Cross
http://www.ncf.carleton.ca/ip/health/redcross/crc/history
A brief text on the origins and development of this organization in Canada and the role played by Surgeon-Major George Sterling Ryerson of the Canadian Army Medical Services.

Hudson's Bay Company

- **Main**: http://www.hbc.com/english.asp

Founded in 1670, the HBC is still alive and functioning today. Find out what ventures the company is currently involved in, or read about HBC history.

- **History**: http://www.hbc.com/hbchistory/

From its founding in 1670 through the early explorers, adventurers and *voyageurs* through the 20th century. Learn about what life was like in the early days, before "Canada" existed.

Hudson Bay Company Fur Trading in 1800s
http://gurukul.ucc.american.edu/TED/HUDSON.HTM
Part of the Trade and Environment Database Project of cases, which seek to provide a common basis for researchers and policy makers to understand issues of trade and the environment. This case study looks at the effects of the Hudson's Bay Company's exploitation of the fur trade in the first half of the 18th century and its impact on the environment.

Libraries Today
http://www.uoguelph.ca/~lbruce/
Dedicated to the history of Canadian public libraries and librarians, especially in the province of Ontario, including biography, public library administration; the impact of technological innovation; rural and children's services, the influence of large urban libraries and the professionalization of librarianship.

Mountain Men and the Fur Trade
http://www.xmission.com/~drudy/amm.html
An online resource center dedicated to the history, traditions and way of life of the trappers, traders and explorers engaged in the fur trade. Includes a "library" of online or downloadable books and articles, an online archive of fur trade documents, images of period artifacts, a gallery of artwork, bibliography and links to a mailing list and other resources.

Northwest Brigade Club
http://www.agt.net/public/gottfred/nwbc.html
A group dedicated to the living history of the western Canadian fur trade from 1774 to 1821. Includes an index, sample articles and subscription info on the quarterly *Northwest Journal.*

Significant Dates in Canadian Railway History
http://infoweb.magi.com/~churcher/candate/candate.htm
Important events and accomplishments in rail travel and transportation from 1790 to 1998.

West Coast Shipbuilding
http://www.schoolnet.ca/collections/shipbuilding/wcssp.htm
A multi-faceted history of the Burrand Dry Dock, later known as Versatile Pacific Shipyards, its role in the development of the Canadian West Coast and contribution to both World Wars.

Geographical History and Information

Canadian Geographic Names [English & French]
http://GeoNames.NRCan.gc.ca/
The source for information on over 350,000 official and formerly official place names in Canada. Find the location of a current or historical place, and generate simple location maps.

Facts on Canada – Geography [English & French]
http://www.infocan.gc.ca/facts/geography-e.html
This site contains an overview of the geographical scope and features of Canada, including a look at each of the seven distinct geographical regions that make up the country.

Historical Atlas of Canada: Data Dissemination Project
http://www.geog.utoronto.ca/hacddp/hacpage.html
Supplemental charts and tabular data to *Volume II: The Land Transformed, 1800-1891.*

Historical Maps of Canada
http://www.sscl.uwo.ca/assoc/acml/faclist.html
A collection of facsimile maps from the Association of Canadian Map Libraries and Archives, from the 1556 "La Nuova Francia" by G. Gastaldi and G.B. Ramusio to a 1920 map of Edmonton West of the 4th Meridian by the Office of the Surveyor General.

National Atlas of Canada [English & French]
http://ellesmere.ccm.emr.ca/english/home-english.html
Contains links to the Resources Atlas, Geography Class, Canadian Community Atlas, BioMap, Spatial Resources and other sources of geographical and demographic data.

Territorial Evolution of Canada
http://www-nais.ccm.emr.ca/schoolnet/issues/terrevol/english/eTerrEvol.html
Maps, from 1867 to 1949, showing the evolution of Canada's international, provincial and territorial boundaries.

Regional History

Acadiensis
http://www.unb.ca/web/arts/History/Acadiensis/index.html
A scholarly journal devoted to research in the history of Atlantic Canada. The journal publishes articles on History, Geography, Political Science, Folklore, Literature, Sociology, Economics and other areas. Information on subscriptions, submissions and the scope of the publication.

For the Life of the World: Charisma and Service of the Missionary Oblates
http://www.pma.edmonton.ab.ca/human/folklife/oblates/cover.htm
An online presentation by the Provincial Museum of Alberta on the life, service and impact of the Oblates of Mary Immaculate on the colonization and culture of the Canadian West.

North: Landscape of the Imagination [English & French]
http://www.nlc-bnc.ca/north/
An online presentation from the National Library of Canada on the history and evolution of the Canadian North, including the pre-contact period, early history, the first half of the 20th century and the modern era.

Cultural Groups

African Canadian Historical Web Site ("Historical Connexion")
http://www.torweb.com/histcon/main.html
Sections include Historical Feature, Genealogy, Historical Images, Books & Videos, Kids & Teachers Corners and more, all showcasing the contributions of African men and women.

Canadian Quaker History
http://home.interhop.net/~aschrauwe/CanHis.html
An historical overview, abridged from the "Canadian Yearly Meeting Discipline."

Cartes des Origines Ethniques des Canadiens, 1901 [French only – maps]
http://www.uottawa.ca/~fgingras/doc/c1901index.html
A series of maps from the 1901 Atlas of Canada, presented in French, showing the ethnic origins of Canadians. Includes maps for Nova Scotia, Cape Breton Island, Prince Edward Island, New Brunswick, three maps for Québec and four maps for Ontario.

The Chinese in Canada: Past and Present
http://www.interlog.com/~fccs/slides.htm
Sections include Historical Background, Cultural Aspects, The Chinese Community Today, Challenges to the Community and a bibliography for further reading.

Doukhobor Home Page
http://www.dlcwest.com/~r.androsoff/index.htm
A source of information on Doukhobor history and culture. Sections include Who are the Doukhobors?, Timeline of Doukhobor History, Culture and Tradition, Events Calendar, etc.

The French Presence in Canada and in British Columbia
http://www.corp.direct.ca/news/french/french1.shtml
An overview of the French and francophone contributions to and achievements in Canada, from Jacques Cartier and Acadia through New France and expansion of the country to the West.

Internment of Ukrainians in Canada 1914-1920
http://www.infoukes.com/history/internment/
A series of articles and photographs recounting the story of the internment of thousands of "enemy aliens," including Ukrainians during the World War I period.

Jewish Communities of the World: Canada
http://www.virtual.co.il/communities/wjcbook/canada/index.htm
A brief look at the demography, history, culture and education, religious life and sites of the Jewish community in Canada.

Mennonites in Canada
http://www.lib.uwaterloo.ca/MHSC/
Includes "Who are the Mennonites," which describes Mennonite beliefs, differences between Mennonite groups, and information on communities in Canada. Also includes The Canadian Mennonite Encyclopedia, a searchable source of information on Mennonite history, statistics, biography, education, the arts and family history.

Métis Development and the Canadian West
http://schoolnet2.carleton.ca/english/ext/aboriginal/metis-de/index.html
A presentation (with text and photos) of the book *Contrasting Worlds*, depicting the Métis' role in the West, from the fur trade and European settlement to the uprisings and confederation.

Testimony of the Canadian Fugitives
http://history.cc.ukans.edu/carrie/docs/texts/canadian_slaves.html
The recorded testimony of escaped slaves in Upper Canada in the mid 1850's.

Ukrainians in Canada: A Selective Bibliography
http://www.civilization.ca/membrs/biblio/bibgrph/ukrbibe.html
Books and articles on Ukrainians available at the Canadian Museum of Civilization's library.

Canadian Women's History

Canadian Chronology of Women's History
http://142.3.223.54/~maguirec/chron.html
A timeline of important events in the history of women's contributions, achievements and rights in Canada, from the arrival of Jeanne Mance in 1641 through the installation of Lenna Bradbum as Canada's first woman police chief at Guelph, Ontario in 1994.

The Canadian Suffrage Movement
http://www.gov.edmonton.ab.ca/parkrec/fort/1905/cansuff.html
A brief look at the effort to secure the right to vote for women in Canada, from the first organized movement in the 1870's and the arguments involved in the historical debate.

Facts on Canada: Women [English & French]
http://www.infocan.gc.ca/facts/women-e.html
This site takes a look at some of the changes in women's rights in Canada since suffrage was won in 1918, including Women and Economy, Women and Government, Women as Activists and Looking Ahead. Presented by InfoCan.

High Flyers: Canadian Women in Aviation [English & French]
http://www.schoolnet.ca/collections/high_flyers/
An online presentation of a past exhibit at the National Aviation Museum featuring the accomplishments of Canadian women in the field of aviation. Features personal photos, memorabilia, archival documents and biographies of 22 women aviators.

Women's Exhibition: Celebrating Women's Achievements
http://www.nlc-bnc.ca/digiproj/women/ewomen.htm
Presentations from the National Library of past Women's History Month exhibitions. Includes women from the Canadian book trade, legislatures, librarianship and music and literature.

Women in Canadian History
http://www.niagara.com/~merrwill/
Brief historical sketches of women who contributed in various ways to Canada's development.

Women in the War – World War II
http://www.valourandhorror.com/DB/ISSUE/Women/index.htm
This site examines the various roles played by Canadian women in World War II. Sections include Servicewomen, At Home, Overseas, Stories, German Women and Nurses.

Canadian Culture, Traditions and Symbols

Canadian Crests and Coats of Arms
http://www.schoolnet.ca/collections/governor/heraldry/index.html
A description of the tradition of heraldry in Canada, with examples of crests and coats of arms for various provinces, first peoples, municipalities, businesses, churches and other groups.

Canadian Recipe Collection
http://sunsite.auc.dk/recipes/english/cat70.html
A collection of several traditional recipes from all across Canada, including Québec Tourtière, Potato Scones, Cape Breton Oatcakes, Nanaimo Bars, Saskatoon Pie and All-Canadian Coffee.

Heroes of Lore and Yore: Canadian Heroes in Fact and Fiction [English & French]
http://www.nlc-bnc.ca/heroes/econtent.htm
Biographical and historical information on several Canadian national heroes, both real and fictional. Portraits include Jeanne Mance, Sir Alexander Mackenzie, Madeleine de Verchères, Anne of Green Gables, Terry Fox, Johnny Canuck and even Sasquatch.

Hold on to Your Hats! History and Meaning of Headwear in Canada
http://www.civilization.ca/membrs/canhist/hats/hat00eng.html
An online exhibit from the Museum of Civilization on the historic and cultural use of hats in Canadian society. Sections include Protection and Practicality, Religion and Ritual, Authority and Status, Identity and Belonging, Fashion and Image, Hat Lore, a Photo Gallery and Game.

Our National Anthem [English & French]
http://www.infocan.gc.ca/facts/anthem.html
The text and a brief history of "O Canada!" Presented by InfoCan: Facts on Canada.

Family Associations & Surnames

Ancestors Found! Surname Registry
http://members.xoom.com/mygenes/lost/resc.htm
A browseable list of surnames that others are researching or posting queries about.

Canada GenWeb Queries

- **Archived**: http://www.rootsweb.com/~canwgw/queryweb/
- **Post/Current**: http://www.geocities.com/Heartland/6625/cgwquery.html

Canada's Query Web
http://www.rootsweb.com/~canwgw/queryweb/
An archive of all queries that have been posted on Canadian GenWeb sites for three months.

GEchanges [English & French]
http://GEchanges-Canada.hypermart.net/index_en.html
A "genealogical classified ads service" for each province in Canada.

Gendex WWW Genealogical Index
http://www.gendex.com/gendex/
This site claims to index genealogical information from hundreds of databases containing information on over five million individuals.

Genealogical Database Index
http://www.gentree.com/
An index of searchable databases on the Web dealing with specific surnames or families.

Northeast Surnames
http://members.mint.net/mdenis/surnames.html
A query bulletin board for surnames of families located in the New England states of the United States and eastern provinces of Canada, including the Maritimes and Québec.

RootsWeb Surname List
http://www.rootsweb.com/rootsweb/searches/rslsearch.html
An index of submitted surnames being researched by amateur genealogists, containing dates and places and contact information for the person submitting the information.

Surname Helper Home Page
http://cgi.rootsweb.com/surhelp/
Surname-indexes participating genealogy Web sites, allowing users to search for a particular surname and its Soundex variants.

Nationalities and Cultural Groups

Hutterite Genealogy: Founding Families: Churchbook Extractions
http://feefhs.org/hut/hff-2.html
Genealogies of some of the founding families of Hutterites that settled in Manitoba, Saskatchewan, Alberta and the western United States.

Irish-Canadian Surname List
http://www.bess.tcd.ie/roots/irishcan.htm
A compilation of submitted data with names of Irish immigrants and locations in Ireland and Canada. Searchable by surname, date and location in Ireland and Canada.

Irish Ancestors
http://www.irish-times.com/ancestor/
Sections on surnames, place names, emigration and a guide to available records.

Individual Surnames and Family Associations

Derrick: http://www.labs.net/ATTFIELD/DERRICKS/

Clan **Fraser** Society of Canada:
http://www.canlinks.com/cdnclanfraser/

Clan **Gunn** Society of North America:
http://www.citynet.net/personal/gunn/clan.html

Harmer Family Association:
http://www.angelfire.com/wa/harmer1/index.html

Lacombe: http://www.cpcug.org/user/jlacombe/

Clan **Macrae**: http://calgary.shaw.wave.ca/~lmcrae/

Clan **Menzies** Society of Canada:
http://home.sprynet.com/sprynet/cmsoc/

Chat Rooms and Mailing Lists

(See Notes section for mailing list instructions)

American-Revolution Mailing List (Also includes French & Indian Wars)

- **all**: american-revolution-l-request@rootsweb.com
- **digest**: american-revolution-d-request@rootsweb.com

Atlantic-Province Mailing List:
majordomo@listserv.northwest.com
all: subscribe atlantic-province@listserv.northwest.com
digest: subscribe atlantic-province-digest@listserv.northwest.com

Brother's Keeper (Software) Mailing List: BK5L-REQUEST@EMCEE.COM

Canada-L: (political, social, cultural, economic)
listserv@vm1.mcgill.ca
`SUBSCRIBE CANADA-L firstname lastname`

Canada Orange Mailing List (Orangemen History, Genealogy, Culture)
http://members.tripod.com/~firstlight_2/canorange.htm

Canadian Archives Mailing List (ARCAN-L):
majordomo@majordomo.srv.ualberta.ca
subscribe ARCAN-L firstname lastname

Canadian Roots-L: listserv@listserv.indiana.edu
SUB CANADIAN ROOTS-L firstname lastname

Colonial-America Mailing List (Early Canadian history also an appropriate topic.)
majordomo@listserv.northwest.com
all: subscribe Colonial-America;
digest: subscribe Colonial-America-digest

Dutch Heritage Mailing List (SHAKEL-NL):
majordomo@esosoft.com
`subscribe schakel-nl`

Genealogy Forum Channel on IRC
http://GEchanges-Canada.hypermart.net/index_en.html
A genealogy chat room on Internet Relay Chat, complete with instructions on installation and use, etiquette, lists of surnames and tips on how to find ancestors and exchange info.

German-Canadian Mailing List
- **all**: german-canadian-l-request@rootsweb.com
- **digest**: german-canadian-d-request@rootsweb.com (digest mode).

Huguenot Mailing List
- **all**: huguenot-l-request@rootsweb.com;
- **digest**: huguenot-d-request@rootsweb.com

Indian Roots Mailing List: maiser@rmgate.pop.indiana.edu
sub indian-roots

Irish-Canadian Mailing List
- **all**: irish-canadian-l-request@rootsweb.com
- **digest**: irish-canadian-d-request@rootsweb.com

H-Canada Discussion List (Canadian History)
- **info**: http://www.h-net.msu.edu/~canada/
- **English subscription**: http://www.usask.ca/history/form4.html
- **Abonnement français**: http://www.usask.ca/history/form5.html

Loyalists-In-Canada Mailing List:
maiser@rmgate.pop.indiana.edu
sub LOYALISTS-IN-CANADA

Surnames-Canada
- **all**: surnames-canada-m-request@rootsweb.com
- **digest**: surnames-canada-l-request@rootsweb.com
- **index**: surnames-canada-i-request@rootsweb.com

20th Century Wars Genealogy Mailing List:
listserv@listserv.indiana.edu
SUB WW20-ROOTS-L firstname lastname

Alberta

Genealogical, Historical and Cultural Societies

Alberta Genealogical Society
http://www.compusmart.ab.ca/abgensoc/
Information on membership, library resources and hours, courses and workshops and the society's Master Name Index, a compilation of information from burial records and cemetery transcriptions, published birth, marriage and death notices, and local history books. Branches:

- **Brooks & District Branch**:
  http://www.eidnet.org/local/bburrows/bbags/
- **Fort McMurray Branch**:
  http://www.tnc.com/tncn/fmgs/ft_main.htm
- **Grande Prairie & District Branch:**
  http://www.telusplanet.net/public/turnbl/ags/gpbranch.html
  Includes information about the society's research assistance service, obituary file, cemetery records and links to full-text versions of the newsletter *Heritage Seekers*.
- **Lethbridge & District Branch**:
  http://www.telusplanet.net/public/turnbl/ags/interests.html

Alberta GenWeb Project
http://www.geocities.com/Heartland/Hills/3508/albertagenweb.html
Links to genealogical information for the districts and counties of the province, much of it indexed in this work. Many districts are under construction or "*temporary*" pages.

Links to Your Canadian Past

Ontario and the Western Provinces

Alberta Family Histories Society

http://www.calcna.ab.ca/afhs/

Information on membership benefits, getting started, meetings, beginners' sessions, society projects, special interest groups, conferences and events. Also includes information on and subject listing of the quarterly journal *Chinook*, plus research info.

Alberta Historical Resources Foundation

http://www.gov.ab.ca/mcd/more/abc/ahrf/ahrf.htm

A Crown Agency attached to the Ministry of Community Development that provides assistance to community heritage projects with partial sponsorships from its Alberta Lotteries allocation.

American Historical Society of Germans From Russia – Calgary Chapter

http://www.ahsgr.org/calgary.html

The society seeks to promote a better understanding of the history of Germans from Russia and to preserve their culture through their descendants. Links to other chapters in the United States and information on obtaining the society's newsletter.

Chinook County Historical Society

http://www.cadvision.com/chinookh/

Membership info, events, and the society's latest newsletter online.

Germans From Russia Heritage Society – Alberta Chapter

http://www.grhs.com/alberta.html

The society seeks to unite those people descended from German-Russian heritage who settled in the Canadian West. Contacts and activities are listed, the society's newsletter is online and information on the society's genealogy research is included.

Icelandic National League of North America: Alberta Chapter Index
http://users.imag.net/~sry.rasgeirs/INL-NewsEventsAB.html
Links to the Norðurljós, Edmonton Icelandic Society; Calgary - Leif Eiriksson Icelandic Society; Markerville - Stephansson Icelandic Society and Evelyn Johannson, Alberta's Fjallkona.

Prince Albert Indian Métis Friendship Centre
http://www.CityLightsNews.com/paimfc.htm
Providing classes, a newsletter and various events for the Métis/aboriginal community.

Sociétié Acadien d'Alberta [English & French]
http://www.connect.ab.ca/~acadie/index.htm
Basic information on the society, its activities and Acadian history.

La Société Généalogique du Nord-Ouest
http://www.genweb.net/~pbg/sgno.htm
The society seeks to assist all persons interested in the genealogy and family history of French Canadian descendants and develop a suitable center for genealogical research.

Société Historique et Généalogique du Smoky River [English & French]
http://www.telusplanet.net/public/genealfa/
The largest francophone genealogical and historical center west of Winnipeg. The site details the society's mission, extensive resources and services, with contact information.

Links to Your Canadian Past

Ontario and the Western Provinces

Archives

Directories

Alphabetical Index to Archival Institutions – Archives Society of Alberta

http://www.glenbow.org/asa/archlist.htm

A listing of member institutions of the ASA, with information on location and holdings.

Map of Alberta's Archival Institutions

http://www.glenbow.org/asa/map.htm

A clickable map of Alberta, showing the locations of archive centers throughout the province, returning a list of archives at a location with information about each center.

Archives Network of Alberta – Database Search

http://library.ubc.ca/WWW.asa.archaa/access+DBASE.ARCHAA

Browse or search the over 5,000 descriptions of the fonds-level and collection-level records in collections throughout the province.

Interprovincial Archival Union List

http://www.CdnCouncilArchives.ca/icaul.html

Search both the British Columbia Archival Union List and the Archives Network of Alberta.

Archive Centers

City of Calgary Archives

http://www.gov.calgary.ab.ca/78/78000rba.html#ARCHIVES

Provides only basic information for locating and contacting the archives.

City of Edmonton Archives
http://www.gov.edmonton.ab.ca/parkrec/archives/
Describes the various printed government and personal records, oral history tapes, maps, photographs, sound recordings, computer records, correspondence, personal histories, diaries and other materials that can be found at the archives.

Glenbow Archives
http://www.glenbow.org/archives.htm
This site gives information on the genealogical research services, archives collections and exhibits. The entire catalogue is searchable, and there are numerous finding aids for the materials located in the collections of the archives for families, individuals and organizations.

Provincial Archives of Alberta
http://www.gov.ab.ca/~mcd/mhs/paa/paa.htm
This site describes the extent and scope of the holdings of the archives and features guides to using the archives, services available, hours and contact information.

Historical Archives (Canadian) at the University of Calgary Library
http://www.ucalgary.ca/library/SpecColl/histarc.htm
Part of the library's Special Collections department, the Historical Archives collection houses many historical documents and collections relating to the province and prominent individuals. Links describing each document/collection in detail are provided.

Museum of the Regiments: Research Archives – Calgary
http://www.nucleus.com/~regiments/research.html
A description of the materials available on the military history of Calgary and Alberta.

United Church Archives Network – Alberta and Northwest Conference Archives
http://www.uccan.org/archives/alberta.htm
Holds pre-1925 records for the Methodist, Presbyterian and Congregational churches and post-1925 records for the United Church of Canada for the entire province of Alberta.

University of Alberta Archives
http://www.ualberta.ca/ARCHIVES/
In addition to housing extensive materials about the history of the university, its affiliated institutions and faculty, the archives also contains information about notable individuals and organizations in provincial and federal politics, western settlement and more.

Whyte Museum Archives and Library
http://www.whyte.org/collections/archives/index.html
Contains materials created in or pertaining to the area bounded by the 49th parallel, Peace River, Front Ranges and Columbia Mountains. Includes over 600 fonds and collections with a focus on mountain areas, biography, culture, family life, transportation and several other subject areas.

Professional Organization

Archives Society of Alberta
http://www.glenbow.org/asa/home.htm
The ASA is an organization devoted to providing a provincial forum for those who work in and are interested in archives. The society is involved in professional development and training and conducts workshops and publishes a newsletter (available online).

Libraries and Research Centers

Directories and Catalogs

Alberta Provincial Government Libraries
http://www.gov.ab.ca:80/library/
Listings (by name or location) of libraries maintained by the provincial government of Alberta.

HYTELNET Library Catalogs: Alberta
http://moondog.usask.ca/hytelnet/ca0/AB.html
Links to libraries in Alberta with telnet connections to their catalogs, with instructions.

Library Websites and Catalogues – Alberta
http://www.nlc-bnc.ca/canlib/ealta.htm
Provided by the National Library of Canada, this site is a list of alphabetical links to the libraries throughout the province and, where applicable, links to their online catalogues.

NEOS Library Consortium
http://www.augustana.ab.ca/neos/
A central Alberta library consortium that maintains The Gate, a shared online catalogue of materials and provides user services to its clients. Links to member institutions.

Libraries and Research Centers

Calgary Library Local History Collection
http://public-library.calgary.ab.ca/words/lochist.htm
Information on the location, contact information, hours and collection of the Local History Collection of the Calgary Public Library, with some local history stories online.

Links to Your Canadian Past

Ontario and the Western Provinces

Edmonton Public Library: Genealogy and Local History Sources
http://libris.publib.edmonton.ab.ca/genealogy/Sources_at_EPL.htm
An overview of the collection, with links to further descriptions of source materials.

Lethbridge Family History Center (Latter Day Saints)
http://www.leth.net/fhc/
Provides a great deal of information on Alberta History, Native History and Pioneer History. The Resources of the FHC are listed in detail, and a comprehensive guide on How to Begin Family History Research is also included.

Okotoks Family History Center (Latter Day Saints)
http://www.cadvision.com/johansss/oktitle.htm
Details the collections and services offered at the library, plus patrons' Tiny Tables.

University of Calgary Library Genealogy Resources
http://www.ucalgary.ca/library/subjects/genealogy/gene.html
Contains information about the book collections, map library, special collections (prairie and local histories, early exploration records), periodical literature, newspapers and microfilm/microfiche collections of genealogical or historical interest in the library.

Professional Organization

The Alberta Library
http://www.library.ualberta.ca/altalib/
A province-wide multitype library consortium dedicated to providing Albertans with barrier-free access to the materials and information resources in all libraries. Educational & training events.

Birth, Marriage, Death, Census and Other Data Online

Vital Statistics and Parish Records

Alberta Registries: Vital Statistics
http://www.gov.ab.ca/ma/reg/vs/vsmain.htm
Official provincial information on birth, marriage, death and adoption records. Also includes information on genealogical searches and locations of the Vital Statistics offices.

Alberta Vital Records
http://www.familytreemaker.com/00000154.html
Contact information on where to write or call for vital records information in Alberta.

Births, Marriages and Deaths Reported in Calgary Newspapers (1883-1899)
http://www.calcna.ab.ca/afhs/news.html
An index to events published in the *Calgary Herald Weekly*, *Calgary Herald Daily* and *Calgary Tribune* for the period indicated. Compiled by the Alberta Family Histories Society.

Cemetery Information

Alberta Cemetery Index Listings
http://www.calcna.ab.ca/afhs/cemetery.html
This index provides basic information on monument and burial information for a great number of cemeteries that surround Calgary.

Cemetery Project: Alberta – Association of Jewish Genealogical Societies
http://www1.jewishgen.org/cemetery/canalber.htm
Information on the Jewish cemeteries and synagogues of southern Alberta.

Aldersyde – Mount View Mennonite Cemetery Index
http://www.calcna.ab.ca/afhs/cemetery/mtview.html
A list of persons buried in this cemetery, with birth and death dates.

Banff Cemetery Index
http://www.calcna.ab.ca/afhs/cemetery/banff_a.html

Black Diamond – Foothills Cemetery Index
http://www.calcna.ab.ca/afhs/cemetery/foothills.html
Alphabetical list of interments, with birth and death dates given.

Blackie – Blackie Cemetery Index
http://www.calcna.ab.ca/afhs/cemetery/blackie.html
Birth and death dates are listed for persons buried in this cemetery.

Burtonsville Cemetery
http://www.geocities.com/Heartland/Hills/3508/countysites/parkland/burtonsvillecemetery.html
An index of burials in this cemetery, with birth and death dates.

Calgary – Burnsland Cemetery Index
http://www.calcna.ab.ca/afhs/cemetery/burns_a.html
Alphabetical listings of interments at this cemetery, with birth and death dates.

Calgary – Springbank Cemetery Index
http://www.calcna.ab.ca/afhs/cemetery/springbk.html
Birth and death dates are listed for persons buried in this cemetery.

Carbon

- **Bethel Baptist Cemetery**:
  http://pixel.cs.vt.edu/library/cemeteries/canada/link/bethelba.txt
- **German Baptist Freudental Cemetery**:
  http://pixel.cs.vt.edu/library/cemeteries/canada/link/freudent.txt

A list of burials for each cemetery, with birth and death dates transcribed from grave markers.

Carstairs Cemetery Index
http://www.calcna.ab.ca/afhs/cemetery/carst_a.html
Birth and death dates are given for individuals buried in this cemetery.

Cochrane – St. Mary's Roman Catholic Cemetery Index
http://www.calcna.ab.ca/afhs/cemetery/stmary.html
A list of burials as well as birth and death dates for those interred at St. Mary's.

Crowsnest Pass – Cemetery Index for Bellevue, Blairmore, Coleman, Cowley, Frank, Hillcrest, Lille, Lundbreck, and Passburg.
http://www.calcna.ab.ca/afhs/cemetery/crows_a.html
A composite index covering the town of Crowsnest Pass and surrounding communities.

Didsbury Cemetery Index
http://www.calcna.ab.ca/afhs/cemetery/dids_a.html
An alphabetical index, with birth and death dates, of individuals buried in the cemetery.

Edmonton – Searching for a Family Member in Our Cemeteries
http://www.gov.edmonton.ab.ca/parkrec/cemetery/search.htm
Alphabetical files containing the names of close to 60,000 people buried in Edmonton municipal cemeteries more than 25 years.

Exshaw – Exshaw Cemetery Index
http://www.calcna.ab.ca/afhs/cemetery/exshaw.html
A list of burials as well as birth and death dates for those interred in this cemetery.

Faith – Sacred Heart Cemetery
http://pixel.cs.vt.edu/library/cemeteries/canada/link/faith.txt
A list of burials with birth and death dates, where known.

Granum Cemetery Index
http://www.calcna.ab.ca/afhs/cemetery/granum_a.html
List of burials for this cemetery, including birth and death dates.

Hespero Cemetery
http://www.genealogia.org/emi/emi41dr.htm
A list of (apparently) Finnish burials in this cemetery, with birth and death dates and notes.

High River – Highwood Cemetery Index
http://www.calcna.ab.ca/afhs/cemetery/high_a.html
An alphabetical listing of interments, with birth and death dates given for individuals.

Hilda Baptist Cemetery
http://pixel.cs.vt.edu/library/cemeteries/canada/link/hilda1.txt
A short history of this cemetery for German-speaking immigrants, with list of names.

Kuusano Cemetery
http://www.genealogia.org/emi/emi41cr.htm
A list of (apparently) Finnish burials in this cemetery, with birth and death dates and notes.

Millarville – Christ Church Cemetery Index
http://www.calcna.ab.ca/afhs/cemetery/cchurch.html
Index of burials, with the individual's name, birth and death dates.

Namaka – Namaka Mennonite Cemetery Index
http://www.calcna.ab.ca/afhs/cemetery/namaka.html
List of the names of those buried in this cemetery, plus birth and death dates, when known.

Okotoks Cemeteries Index
http://www.calcna.ab.ca/afhs/cemetery/okotok_a.html
Index, with birth and death dates, of burials in the town's cemeteries.

Stavely –St. Vincent Roman Catholic Cemetery Index
http://www.calcna.ab.ca/afhs/cemetery/stavely.html
Alphabetical list of burials for this cemetery, including birth and death dates of individuals.

Census Information

Index to the 1891 Dominion Census – Lethbridge Sub-district, Alberta, Northwest Territories
http://mypage.direct.ca/d/dobee/lethmain.html
2,842 names in the area from Lethbridge south to the U.S. border. Original page references.

Land Records

Alberta Registries: Land Titles Services Information Page
http://www.gov.ab.ca/ma/reg/lt/ltmain.htm
Includes an overview of the Land Titles Offices and information on fees and how to obtain copies of land title records, as well as requesting plan, name or general register searches.

Museums/Historic Sites & Groups

Directory

Alberta Museums and Historic Sites
http://www.gov.ab.ca/~mcd/mhs/mhs.htm
Presented by Alberta Community Development, this site provides links to information on sites throughout the province, many of which don't have their own Web sites.

Museums and Historic Sites

Alberta Railway Museum – Northeast Edmonton, AB
http://www.discoveredmonton.com/RailwayMuseum/
Featuring working steam and diesel locomotives, old freight and passenger cars, etc.

Bar U Ranch National Historic Site – Longview, AB [English & French]
http://parkscanada.pch.gc.ca/parks/alberta/bar_u_ranch/bar_u_ranche.htm
An historic ranch in Alberta's foothills, commemorating the history and importance of ranching in the province. 35 buildings and structures, including a Visitor's Centre, barns, log cabin, etc.

Bonnyville and District Museum – Bonnyville, AB
http://www.town.bonnyville.ab.ca/museum.html
Displays honoring the Native, French and Ukrainian contributions to the history of the area, including re-created log church, fur trader's shack, schoolhouse and other early buildings.

Calgary Heritage Park – Calgary, AB
http://www.heritagepark.org/
Stroll through this re-created 1910 town, including pioneer homes, schoolhouse, RNWMP barracks, a hotel, shops and businesses, trains and costumed interpreters.

Calgary and Edmonton Railway Museum – Edmonton, AB
http://www.discoveredmonton.com/RailMuseum/
Exhibits detailing the role of the railroad in bringing pioneers, settlers and immigrants to Alberta.

Fort Calgary Historic Park – Calgary, AB
http://www.fortcalgary.ab.ca/
A 40-acre park commemorating the history from the founding of the North West Mounted Police Fort in 1875 to the development of the city of Calgary. The site includes an Interpretive Centre, reconstruction of the fort, the Hunt House Historic Site and the Deane House Historic Site.

Fort Edmonton Project – University of Alberta
http://uglab.phys.ualberta.ca/web/FortEdmWebSite/FortEdmonton.html
Information on the archaeological investigation into one of Alberta's early fur trading forts.

Fort George-Buckingham House Site Profile – Elk Point, AB
http://www.agt.net/public/gottfred/bhfghsp.html
An article from the Northwest Journal profiling this site, which presents two fur trading posts that operated between 1792 and 1801, along with an interpretive center.

Fort MacLeod Museum (The Fort Museum) – Fort MacLeod, AB
http://www.discoveralberta.com/FortMuseum/
The official museum of the North West Mounted Police. Features artifacts from everyday Mountie life, Indian artifacts and reconstructions of two original buildings...and horses!

Fort Whoop-up Interpretive Centre – Lethbridge, AB

- http://susan.chin.gc.ca:8016/BASIS/guide/user/search/DDW?M=1&U=1&W=GUIDE_KEY=1274
- http://netreader.com/community/lethbridge/stories/historical/whoop.html

Frank Slide Interpretive Centre – Crowsnest Pass, AB
http://www.frankslide.com/
Displays, programs and presentations highlighting the history of Crowsnest Pass and the Canadian Rockies, featuring the 1903 Frank Slide (rockslide-avalanche), Canadian Pacific Railway, European settlement, early underground coal mining and community life.

Glenbow Museum – Calgary, AB
http://www.glenbow.org/museum.htm
Exhibits on the cultural history, ethnology and military history of the West. Collections contain objects relating to those who explored or settled the area from the late 1800's to the present day, the indigenous people of North America and Canadian and international military history.

Head-Smashed-In Buffalo Jump Interpretive Center – Fort MacLeod, AB
http://www.head-smashed-in.com/
This center depicts the ecology, mythology, lifestyle and technology of Blackfoot peoples, at the world's oldest, largest and best preserved buffalo jump. A UNESCO World Heritage Site.

Heritage Park – Fort McMurray, AB
http://www.schoolnet.ca/collections/fortmc/map.htm
A 6.6-acre facility, with a museum, 15 historic buildings and 10 large artifacts, including railroad cars, tugboat, drill rig, etc. A clickable map shows photos and information on the exhibits.

Jasper-Yellowhead Museum and Archives – Jasper, AB
http://www.jasper-alberta.com/JasperYellowheadMuseumArchives.htm
Dedicated to the history of the inhabitants of and travelers through this mountain corridor area. Exhibits include Fur Trade, Ribbons of Steel, Seekers of Wilderness, Visions of Wilderness and Fitzhugh to Jasper. Archives include books, photographs, manuscripts and histories of the area.

Leduc No. 1 Interpretive Center – Devon, AB
http://www.blackgold.ab.ca/leduc1/
Photos and history of this historic well and the oil industry in the region.

Luxton Museum of the Plains Indian – Banff, AB [English & French]
http://www.schoolnet.ca/collections/luxton/
Exhibits and online presentations of the daily and spiritual life, traditions, ceremonies and history of the Indians of the Northern Plains and Canadian Rockies.

Mackenzie Crossroads Museum and Visitor's Centre – High Level, AB
http://www.town.highlevel.ab.ca/Museum/Museum.htm
A local history museum, presenting over 1,600 food and medicine containers and other artifacts from the 1800's and early 1900's in a trading post/general store setting.

Millet and District Museum and Exhibit Room – Millet, AB
http://susan.chin.gc.ca:8016/BASIS/guide/user/search/DDW?M=1&U=1&W=GUIDE_KEY=1048
Ethno-history museum of Millet and the 13 surrounding school districts.

Musée Héritage Museum – St. Albert, AB
http://susan.chin.gc.ca:8016/BASIS/guide/user/search/DDW?M=1&U=1&W=GUIDE_KEY=1660
Dedicated to preserving St. Albert's historic sites, artifacts and specimens. Includes the Little White School and St. Albert Grain Elevator Park. [*Note*: the museum's new Web site, *http://www.compusmart.ab.ca/museum/*, only had the Callihoo genealogy at press time.]

Museum of the Regiments – Calgary, AB
http://www.nucleus.com/~regiments/
Western Canada's largest military museum, depicting Canadian military history from Calgary's perspective. Made up of four individual museums commemorating the contributions of:

- Lord Strathcona's Horse (Royal Canadians): http://www.nucleus.com/~rdennis/
- Princess Patricia's Canadian Light Infantry: http://www.nucleus.com/~kitshop/museum.html
- The Calgary Highlanders: http://db.nucleus.com/highmus/museum.htm
- The King's Own Calgary Regiment: *no individual site currently online*

An online tour of the Museum of the Regiments is also available at the main Web site.

Naval Museum of Alberta – Calgary, AB
http://www.navalmuseum.ab.ca/
A collection of naval guns and artifacts, including three RCN aircraft.

Provincial Museum of Alberta: Human History Program – Edmonton, AB
http://www.pma.edmonton.ab.ca/human/intro.htm
This site gives information about the various sections of the Human History Program at the museum. The program is divided into two sections: Aboriginal and early contact history (Archaeology and Ethnology) and post-contact history (Folklife, Government History and Western Canadian History).

Remington-Alberta Carriage Centre – Cardson, AB
http://info@remingtoncentre.com/
One of the largest collections of horse-drawn vehicles in North America. The Centre houses over 200 carriages, wagons and sleighs. Includes an online presentation of the facility.

Rocky Mountain House National Historic Site – Rocky Mountain House, AB [English & French]
http://www.worldweb.com/ParksCanada-Rocky/index.html
This site of rival posts of the North West Company and Hudson's Bay Company commemorates the fur trade in the region. Many history articles available online.

The Western Canada Heritage Centre – Cochrane, AB
http://www.whcs.ab.ca/
A cowboy, ranch and rodeo interpretive center dedicated to the cattle industry and the sport of rodeo. Rodeos, hands-on interactive, educational, and interpretive activities & Virtual Tour.

Whyte Museum of the Canadian Rockies – Banff, AB
http://www.whyte.org/
This museum, dedicated to mountain transportation, recreation and the pioneer household houses a Heritage Collection of both "built heritage" (the restored Whyte and Moore houses, etc.) and moveable cultural property relating to pioneer life and mountaineering.

Links to Your Canadian Past
Ontario and the Western Provinces

Professional Organization

Museums Alberta: The Association of Alberta's Museums
http://www.ualberta.ca/MUSEUMS/ALBERTA/
A province-wide organization providing advisory services, an annual conference, professional publications as well as a training and development program for museum workers and volunteers.

Military, Native and Historic Groups

Alberta GenWeb Roll of Honour Project
http://www.geocities.com/Heartland/Hills/3508/genweb/vet.html
A list of Alberta men and women who served in the Boer War, World War I, World War II and the Korean War.

Calgary Highlanders
http://db.nucleus.com/highmus/frames.htm
Includes the history of this Land Reserve Infantry Regiment from 1921 to the present.

Lord Strathcona's Horse (Royal Canadians)
http://www.nucleus.com/~rdennis/
This museum site provides a history of the regiment and its Roll of Honour.

Memories of War, Dreams of Peace: Canadians Abroad
http://www.rdpl.red-deer.ab.ca/memories/memories.html
Information on this exhibit at the Red Deer Museum, and short biographies on some men and women from Alberta who served abroad during World War II.

Métis Nation of Alberta
http://www.metis.org/
Promoting the cultural, economic, educational, political and social rights and needs of Métis in Alberta and Canada. Current events and projects are featured, as is an e-mail directory.

Princess Patricia's Canadian Light Infantry
http://www.nucleus.com/~kitshop/
The history of this regiment and its activities and involvement in Canada and abroad.

Tribes and Bands of Alberta
http://hanksville.phast.umass.edu:8000/cultprop/contacts/tribal/AB.html
Contact information for the different indigenous groups in the province.

Provincial and Local History and Photos

Provincial, Regional and Cultural History and Photos

A **Brief Railway History of Alberta**
http://www.discoveredmonton.com/RailwayMuseum/history.html
From the Canadian Pacific Railway in 1882-83 to the Alberta Resources Railway in the 1950's.

Alberta Historical Timeline
http://www.calcna.ab.ca/afhs/timeline.html
Prominent events and accomplishments marking the province from 1754 to 1995.

Alberta Between the Wars, 1919-1939: The Photographs of William J. Oliver
http://www.schoolnet.ca/collections/wjoliver/
Includes photos of The City of Calgary, Alberta Events, Industry in Alberta, Transportation in Alberta, Sports and Outdoor Pursuits, First Nations of Alberta, Military and RCMP, and Geography of Alberta. A biography of Oliver is also included, with comments on the photos.

The Germans From Russia ... In Western Canada
http://www.grhs.com/History2.html
Includes information on why these immigrants chose Canada and where they settled.

Hutterite Colonies in Alberta
http://tor-pw1.netcom.ca/~blongway/hutter.htm
A list of colonies, with year founded, location and name of founding colony.

Hutterite Place Names in North America: 87 Dariusleut Colonies (1973)
http://feefhs.org/hut/h-dplace.html
Includes many colonies in Alberta, with year founded and parent colony.

Métis Nation of Alberta: History
http://www.metis.org/pages/history.html
Includes the history of the Métis flag and sash, as well as the history of Alberta's Métis people.

Southwest Alberta History
http://www.cadvision.com/traces/alta/swapinfo.html#Brief
A brief overview of the history of this area, including the city of Calgary, Foothills MD, Willow Creek MD and Vulcan County.

Local History and Photos

Airdrie – History and Roots of Airdrie
http://www.airdrie.com/text/t_start.htm#history
Information on the naming, settlement and growth of this town, with present-day facts & figures.

Bonnyville:

- **The History of Bonnyville and District**:
  http://www.town.bonnyville.ab.ca/history.html
- **Multi-Cultural Influences**:
  http://www.town.bonnyville.ab.ca/culture.html

Calgary: Yesterday and Today
http://www.gov.calgary.ab.ca/78/78000mh1.html
Part of the City of Calgary Municipal Handbook Online, this article is a brief summary of the history of the city from its origins through its incorporation and growth to today.

Camrose – A Short History of Camrose
http://www.camrose.com/comm/history.htm
From early settlement and missions through the development of the agricultural industry.

Cochrane – More About Cochrane and Area
http://www.town.cochrane.ab.ca/html/more.html
Facts and legends about local sites and geographic features.

Cold Lake Area: History
http://www.ccinet.ab.ca/dsi/coldlake/history.htm
From native settlements to fur traders and the arrival of the RCAF to today.

Edmonton – Historic Tour of Edmonton
http://www.gov.edmonton.ab.ca/planning/histogif.htm
Text and photo history of the city, presented by the Planning and Development department.

Edmonton – History of Edmonton
http://www.infoedmonton.com//history.html
An overview of the city's history and the influence of the fur trade and oil industry.

Edmonton – Historic Background of Forts Edmonton and Augustus
http://uglab.phys.ualberta.ca/web/FortEdmWebSite/history.html
Presented as part of the archaeological research into the former Fort Edmonton, this site gives the background of the two forts, plus an early map of Fort Edmonton from 1864.

Fort McMurray – The History of Fort McMurray [English & French]
http://www.schoolnet.ca/collections/fortmc/
Includes an historical timeline of the town from 1700 to the present day, with photographs.

Fort Saskatchewan History
http://www.city.fort-saskatchewan.ab.ca:1080/fortsask/fortinfo.nsf/c5d29660ad552fc8872564840055d489/4f4d2362ede63c888725647300554f87?OpenDocument
From its beginnings in canoe building and fur trading, through the 1885 Rebellion to today.

Hanna Online History
http://www.town.hanna.ab.ca/townhist.htm
A comprehensive list of articles dealing with the social, economic and cultural history of this town and district, including The Settlers, Pioneer Business, Construction Boom and Schools.

Lethbridge: History of a Prairie Community [English & French]
http://www.schoolnet.ca/collections/prairie/
Part of the SchoolNet Digital Collections, this site presents 8 individual exhibits: Our Railway Ties, Irrigating Southern Alberta, The Story of Agriculture, Mining for Coal, Lethbridge's Military History, The People of Alberta, Society and Culture and Industry and Commerce.

Red Deer – Quick Facts About Red Deer
http://www.city.red-deer.ab.ca/about/about.html
Includes a Brief History of Red Deer, How Red Deer Got Its Name, information on present-day Red Deer, plus the World's Most Boring Post Card and the Official Red Deer Cookie.

Town of Turner Valley History
http://www.town.turner-valley.ab.ca/tturval/history.htm
The story of the development of Turner Valley, birthplace of Alberta's oil and gas industry.

Family Associations/Surnames

Province-wide and Regional Surnames

Alberta Genealogical Society Surname Index
Surname interests of the society's members, with dates, locations contact information.

- **Fort McMurry Branch**: http://www.tnc.com/tncn/fmgs/sur_indx.htm
- **Grande Prairie & District Branch**: http://www.telusplanet.net/public/turnbl/ags/interests.html

Alberta GenWeb Biography Forum
http://cgi.rootsweb.com/~genbbs/genbbs.cgi/Canada/Alberta/GeneralBios
Like a surname query list, this forum allows researchers to post biographies of Alberta settlers and citizens. View or post biographies or browse a list of surnames.

Alberta GenWeb – General Surname Queries, Province of Alberta
http://cgi.rootsweb.com/~genbbs/genbbs.cgi/Canada/Alberta/General
Province-wide or unknown location queries. View, post or browse the surname list.

Alberta GenWeb Regional Sites – Surname Queries and Research Interests
Due to the large number of regional GenWeb sites in Alberta, please visit the regional Web site listed under *Genealogical, Historical and Cultural Societies* for queries and surname interests.

Alberta Surname Interests
http://www.calcna.ab.ca/afhs/memfram.html
A detailed list of the surname interests of the members of the Alberta Family Histories Society, with e-mail addresses of pertinent members. Listings are only of society members, but anyone is welcome to contact listed members about surnames.

Individual Histories of Pioneers Who Helped Settle Southern Alberta
http://www.leth.net/fhc/IND.HTM
This site contains brief histories or stories about pioneers who settled in the province. All information was submitted by individual researchers or family members.

Glenbow Archives Finding Aids
http://www.glenbow.org/archhtm/findaids.htm
Actually a detailed inventory of the archive's records, these aids list the contents of collections and donations given to the archives relating to pioneer individuals and families of Alberta, often containing letters, journals, commissions and photos.

Historical Archives (Canadian) at the University of Calgary Library
http://www.ucalgary.ca/library/SpecColl/histarc.htm
Links describing each document/collection in detail are provided. Many of the documents or materials included directly concern or are the work of prominent citizens of Alberta, including personal and professional artifacts.

Links to Your Canadian Past

Ontario and the Western Provinces

Individual Surnames or Family Associations

Adkins: http://www.familytreemaker.com/users/a/d/k/Kenneth-G-Adkins/GENE0001-0001.html

Baker:http://www.familytreemaker.com/users/b/a/k/Jeffrey--Baker/COL2-0001.html

Bordeleau Families in Alberta
English: http://www.acpo.on.ca/claude/albrta-a.htm;
Français:http://www.acpo.on.ca/claude/albrta-a.htm

Calihoo: Musée Héritage Museum Register Report
http://www.compusmart.ab.ca/museum/RR_IDX/SUR.htm
An in-house genealogy developed for the Calihoo family, with over 15,000 names for researchers of Métis, Aboriginal or Francophone roots in Alberta.

Costello : http://pwaldron.bess.tcd.ie/costello/

Derrick:
http://www.geocities.com/Heartland/Plains/6572/battle.html

Hiron/l'Hirondelle: http://www.familytreemaker.com/users/h/i/r/Don-W-Hiron/COL1-0015.html

Kearns/Cairns: http://www.cadvision.com/traces/kcc/kearns.html

McCormick: http://www.mccormickfamily.com/

McLaren:
http://www.familytreemaker.com/users/m/c/l/Lawrence-L-McLaren/index.html

Nolan : http://pwaldron.bess.tcd.ie/costello/

Pouchée, Pushee, Pushea, Pushie:
http://www.calgary.shaw.wave.ca/~dpushie/

Schuh: http://www.familytreemaker.com/users/b/e/n/Alan--F-Benner/GENE0001-0003.html

Schlaut: http://www.familytreemaker.com/users/s/c/h/Joseph-H-Schlaut/GENE0001-0003.html

Scurfield: http://www.familytreemaker.com/users/s/c/u/Robert-M-Scurfield/ODT2-0001.html

Stiles: http://www.geocities.com/Heartland/Park/2849/

Waylett: http://www.familytreemaker.com/users/w/a/y/Douglas--C-Waylett/ODT2-0006.html

Chat Rooms and Mailing Lists

Alberta Mailing List (Genealogy & History):
majordomo@listserv.northwest.com
all: subscribe alberta;
digest: subscribe alberta-digest

British Columbia

Genealogical, Historical and Cultural Societies

Abbotsford Genealogical Group
http://www3.bc.sympatico.ca/abbotsfordgengroup/AGG.HTML
Information on the society's meetings, library, membership and events.

Black Historical and Cultural Society of British Columbia
http://www.multinova.com/canroots/blackframes/index.htm
Celebrating and preserving Black history in the province. Includes historical photos.

British Columbia Black History Awareness Society – Victoria, BC
http://www.islandnet.com/~bcbhas/index.htm
Sections of the site include History & Education committees, Black History Month, Black Achievements and excerpts from the society's newsletter.

British Columbia Folklore Society
http://www.folklore.bc.ca/
Dedicated to collecting and preserving recordings and artifacts relating to the family, workplace and cultural traditions of the province. The society's newsletter is available online.

British Columbia Genealogical Society
http://www.npsnet.com/bcgs/
Describes the aims, membership benefits and meetings of the BCGS. Provides a catalogue of the society's Resource Centre, a subject index of past newsletters, and a directory of member e-mail addresses, plus upcoming events.

British Columbia GenWeb Project
http://www.islandnet.com/~jveinot/genweb/bcgenweb.html
Links to genealogical information, much of it indexed elsewhere in this volume. Regions:

- **Cariboo-Chilcotin**:
  http://www.geocities.com/SiliconValley/Garage/5414/
- **Southwestern-Vancouver Coast**:
  http://www.geocities.com/Heartland/Hills/1285/
- **Vancouver Island**:
  http://www.geocities.com/Heartland/Acres/5964/

Bulkley Valley Genealogical Society
http://www.hiway16.com/genealogy/index.htm
Information on meetings, events and society contacts.

Campbell River Genealogy Club
http://www.connected.bc.ca/~genealogy/
Information on the club's library, meetings, publications, events and newsletter.

District 69 Historical Society
http://www.macn.bc.ca/~d69hist/
Information about the society, which includes Parksville, Nanoose, Errington, Coombs, Hilliers, French Creek. Tours, displays, meetings, heritage advocacy. Online census information.

Germans from Russia Heritage Society - British Columbia Chapter
http://feefhs.org/grhs/grhs-bc.html

Hallmark Society
http://www.islandnet.com/~helen/Hallmark.html
Advocates the preservation and restoration of heritage buildings as well as natural, cultural and horticultural landmarks in the Capital Regional District (Victoria). Publishes a newsletter.

Heritage Vancouver Society
http://home.istar.ca/~glenchan/hvsintro.shtml
Works towards heritage preservation, excellence in new design and community planning. The society publishes heritage research, conducts walking tours and sponsors heritage exhibits.

Icelandic Canadian Club of British Columbia
http://users.imag.net/~sry.rasgeirs/ICCBC/Welcome.html
Promotes Icelandic culture, traditions and fellowship with language classes, a library and archives, scholarships, events and a monthly newsletter, available online.

Jewish Genealogical Institute of British Columbia
http://www.geocities.com/Heartland/Hills/4441/
Dedicated to helping those of Jewish heritage in the province research their roots and preserve their heritage. The group has a collection of genealogical resources and conducts workshops.

Kamloops Family History Society
http://www.ocis.net/kfhs/
Information on the society's meetings, published indexes and local genealogical resources.

Kelowna and District Genealogical Society
http://www.wkpowerlink.com/~gjespers/kdgs.html
For researchers in the Okanagan Valley. Info on the library, classes and publications available.

Nanaimo Family History Society
- http://www.island.net/~tghayes/
- http://www.sd68.nanaimo.bc.ca/nol/community/famhist.htm

Information on membership, meetings and the society's vital statistics/cemetery indexes.

Nanaimo Historical Society
http://www.sd68.nanaimo.bc.ca./nol/community/nhistsoc.htm
Basic information on the society, with contacts.

Okanagan Historical Society
http://www.domain-fx.com/ohs/
The OHS, with its seven member branches, has taken the responsibility for writing and publishing the local history of the Okanagan Valley of British Columbia.

The Slovak Heritage and Cultural Society of British Columbia
http://www.iarelative.com/slovakbc.htm
Information on Slovak arts, crafts, traditions, villages and genealogical research.

Slovenian Genealogical Society: Canada (British Columbia) Chapter
http://www.feefhs.org/slovenia/frgsgsbc.html
Contact information and links to the Slovenian Research List and "Slovenes in Canada."

South Cariboo Genealogy Group
http://www.web-trek.net/stern/cariboo.html
A society encompassing the towns of 100 Mile House, 108 Mile, Lac La Hache, Lone Butte, Bridge Lake and Clinton. Excerpts from past newsletters available online.

South Okanagan Genealogical Society
http://vvalley.net/organizations/special/sogs/index.htm
Contact and meeting information, and an index to the society's newsletter, *Grapevines*.

Valemount Historic Society
http://www.vis.bc.ca/histsoc.htm

Links to Your Canadian Past
Ontario and the Western Provinces

City of Vancouver Heritage Fact Sheets
http://www.city.vancouver.bc.ca/commsvcs/planning/heritage.htm
Extensive information on the Heritage Conservation Foundation, Heritage Register and other city-sponsored initiatives and policies to conserve Vancouver's municipal heritage.

Vancouver Historical Society
http://www.vcn.bc.ca/vhs/
Information on the society's aims, newsletter, meetings, events and historical research service.

Vernon and District Family History Society
http://www.junction.net/vernhist/index.html
Information on the society's meetings, membership, publications and local resources.

Victoria Genealogical Society
http://www.islandnet.com/~vgs/homepage.html
Information on library holdings, special interest groups, meetings, publications and making queries. The Family Histories Collection and Journal Index are searchable.

Victoria Heritage Foundation
http://www.vhf.city.victoria.bc.ca/
Administers the city's heritage restoration and preservation. Operates a house grants program to preserve heritage landmarks, conducts walking tours, and provides heritage guidelines.

Women's History Network
http://rapidnet.bc.ca/~cbartos/
Dedicated to fostering an interest and activity in women's history in British Columbia.

Professional Organizations

British Columbia Historical Federation
http://www.selkirk.bc.ca/bchf/main1.htm
An umbrella organization representing regional societies in the province. The BCHF promotes historic preservation, encourages research and publishes a newsletter and historical studies.

Heritage Society of British Columbia
http://www.islandnet.com/~hsbc/
The HSBC represents approximately 160 groups in the province. Advocates heritage awareness, preservation, legislation and policy. This comprehensive site provides access to the society's newsletter, info on children's education, professional training, conferences and much more.

Archives

Directories

British Columbia Archival Union List
http://www.harbour.com/AABC/bcaul.html
Search the database of descriptions of records at 159 archival institutions throughout the province. Browse by section or search for keywords, with advanced search capabilities.

A **Guide to Archival Repositories in BC**
http://www.harbour.com/AABC/bcguide.html
Browse the 184 provincial repositories alphabetically, by type or with a clickable map. Provides contact, access and holdings info for many centers that don't have their own Web sites.

Interprovincial Archival Union List
http://www.CdnCouncilArchives.ca/icaul.html
Search both the British Columbia Archival Union List and the Archives Network of Alberta.

Archive Centers

British Columbia Archives
http://www.bcarchives.gov.bc.ca/index.htm
Not only details the holdings of the Research Library of the archives, but gives full search capabilities of the nearly 12,000 publications and 38,000 images catalogued online. Visit the "Virtual Reference Room," a clickable map of the archives, for info on each part of the library.

Central Okanagan Records Survey
http://royal.okanagan.bc.ca/cthomson/records_survey/cors/corsfram.html
Online info on the archived records of this district, with headings for Cities, District Municipalities, Libraries, Courts, Indian Organizations, Museums, Private Collections, etc.

Cranbrook Archives, Museum and Landmark Foundation
http://crowsnest.bc.ca/camal/
"Dedicated to the research, preservation, interpretation and exhibition of Cranbrook's heritage, with special emphasis on the history of the railway."

Esquimalt Municipal Archives
http://www.mun.esquimalt.bc.ca/Main/archives.htm
A description of the holdings and services at the archives, with contact information.

Fraser-Fort George Regional Museum Archives – Prince George, BC
http://www.pgonline.com/ffgrm/collecti.htm
Details the holdings of the archival section of the museum, pertaining to the local region.

Nanaimo Community Archives
http://www.sd68.nanaimo.bc.ca/nol/community/nca.htm
Basic contact and holdings information for this community/regional archive center.

New Westminster – Diocese of New Westminster Archives
http://www.vancouver.anglican.ca/diocesnw.htm#archives
Contact information and holdings overview, plus a downloadable request form.

City of Richmond Archives
http://www.city.richmond.bc.ca/archives/archives.html
A very comprehensive site, detailing the municipal records, government publications and oral histories in the archives. Also provides research tools for the biography and reference files and Richmond bibliography and allows online searches of photographic or all resources.

Salt Spring Island Archives
http://web.uvic.ca/history-robinson/archives.html
Information on the collection of materials that relate to the Island and the murder of William Robinson. Government records, newspapers, diaries and other holdings are described.

Simon Fraser University Archives Program
http://www.sfu.ca/archives/archival-prog.html
In addition to university records, SFU houses a collection of records of individuals and organizations as part of its private historical research collections.

South Okanagan-Similkameen Records Survey Table of Contents
http://royal.okanagan.bc.ca/cthomson/records_survey/survtoc3.htm
Online info on the aived records of this district, with headings for Cities, Federal Government, Libraries, Courts, Indian Organizations, Museums, Private Collections, etc.

United Church Archives Network – Alberta and Northwest Conference Archives
http://www.uccan.org/archives/alberta.htm
Pre-1925 records for the Methodist, Presbyterian and Congregational churches and post-1925 records for the United Church for the northeast section of the province, including Zion Church, Chetwynd; Hillcrest Church, Fort Nelson; St. Luke's Church, Fort St. John; St. Peter's Church, Hudson Hope; South Peace Church, Dawson Creek and St. Paul's Church, Tumbler Ridge, BC

United Church of Canada Archives Network - British Columbia Conference Archives
- http://www.uccan.org/archives/britishcolumbia.htm
- http://www.interchange.ubc.ca/bstewart/

Information on the United Church of Canada records retained since 1925 and records of the Methodist, Presbyterian, and Congregational Churches in the province prior to 1925.

City of Vancouver Archives
http://www.city.vancouver.bc.ca/ctyclerk/archives/index.html-ssi
A detailed description of holdings, plus genealogical and other research guides. Search the descriptions of holdings or browse a list of municipal or individual/organization holdings.

City of Victoria Archives and Records Division
- **genealogy research guide**: http://www.city.victoria.bc.ca/archives/genogy.htm
- **main**: http://www.city.victoria.bc.ca/archives/index.htm

Includes a Private Documents Index and guides to house land use research.

Victoria Women's Movement Archives – University of Victoria
http://gateway2.uvic.ca/archives/vwma/home.html
Describes the archives collection and fonds. Also provides access to the UVic Archives catalog.

West Vancouver Memorial Library Historical Photo Archive
http://hp.bccna.bc.ca/Library/WestVan/history/
An online catalogue of historic photos of West Vancouver's growth and development.

Professional Organization

Archives Association of British Columbia
http://www.harbour.com/AABC/
Providing education, publications, project support and advocacy for member institutions.

Libraries and Resource Centers

Directory

Canadian Library Websites and Catalogues: British Columbia
http://www.nlc-bnc.ca/canlib/ebc.htm
A list of public, private and educational library Web sites and catalogues in the province.

HYTELNET Library Catalogs: British Columbia
http://moondog.usask.ca/hytelnet/ca0/BC.html
A list of libraries with telnet connections. Includes login and user information.

Libraries and Research Centers

Doukhobor Collection – University of British Columbia Library
http://library.usask.ca/spcol/collections/047e.html
A description of the collection of materials on immigrants from the former Soviet Union.

Kelowna Branch Family History Library
http://www.wkpowerlink.com/~mold/fhl.htm
Contact information and list of resources available at this LDS family history center.

University of British Columbia Library Special Collections and Archives
http://www.library.ubc.ca/spcoll/
Collections include Rare Books and Special Collections, University Archives and Records Management Services, Cartographic Archives and Historic Maps, Manuscript Collections, Historical Photographs and Graduate Theses.

Vancouver Public Library Central Branch: Special Collections
http://www.vpl.vancouver.bc.ca/branches/LibrarySquare/spe/home.html
Includes the Northwest History Collection, Historical Photographs, City Directories, Vancouver Building Register and rare books. Services include a photo copystand and photo sales.

Vancouver Public Library: History and Government Division
http://www.vpl.vancouver.bc.ca/branches/LibrarySquare/his/home.html
Information on the collections, services, indexes, study guides and a floor plan of the library.

Birth, Marriage, Death, Census and Other Data Online

Vital Statistics and Parish Records

British Columbia Vital Records
http://www.familytreemaker.com/00000155.html
Contact information for obtaining vital records from the province, with holdings.

British Columbia Vital Statistics Agency: Genealogy
http://www.hlth.gov.bc.ca/vs/genealogy/
How to obtain birth, marriage, death and adoption certificates, plus an online index to records.

Death Registration Index
http://www2.bcarchives.gov.bc.ca/cgi-bin/www2vsd
A searchable index of Vital Statistics death registration information for the province for the period 1872-1976. Searchable fields include surname and given name, age, date or place of death, etc. Returns give registration number for the event and microfilm number where the record can be found.

Marriage Indexes: Vital Statistics
http://www2.bcarchives.gov.bc.ca/cgi-bin/www2vsm
A searchable index of Vital Statistics marriage registration information for the province for the period 1872-1921. Any of several fields (names, dates, place) may be entered. Returns give the registration number of the event and microfilm number of the record.

Parksville/Qualicum Area Marriage Notices
http://macn.bc.ca/~d69hist/marriage.html
Mid-Vancouver Island marriages extracted from area newspapers between 1948 and 1994.

Parksville/Qualicum Area Obituaries
http://macn.bc.ca/~d69hist/obits.html
Extracted from area newspapers for deaths between 1948 and 1994.

Vancouver Island Genealogy Photocopy Service
http://www.geocities.com/Heartland/Acres/5964/copies.htm
A fee-based service for obtaining photocopies of archival records on Vancouver Island.

Victims of the 1887 Nanaimo Mine Explosion
http://www.geocities.com/Heartland/Acres/5964/miners.htm

Cemetery Information

British Columbia Cemetery Finding Aid (BCCFA)
http://www.islandnet.com/bccfa/
Browse or search this list of over 100,000 interments from 141 cemeteries across the province. Find the surname, cemetery name and location, then contact the contributing organization.

North Okanagan and Arrow Lakes Valleys Cemetery Inscriptions
http://www.junction.net/vernhist/V4.html
Several cemeteries in the region catalogued by the Vernon and District Family History Society. Individual Cemeteries are indexed below, by location.

Armstrong Spallumcheen Cemetery Inscriptions
http://www.junction.net/vernhist/aarmstrong.html

Barkerville Cemetery
http://www.geocities.com/Heartland/Meadows/9402/barkermi.html
Cemetery history and alphabetized tombstone inscriptions.

Burton

- **Burton Cemetery (new)**:
  http://www.junction.net/vernhist/aburton.html
- **Burton Cemetery (old)**:
  http://www.junction.net/vernhist/aburtold.html

Colstream Cemetery – St. Nicholas Ukrainian Catholic
http://www.junction.net/vernhist/acoldstreamukr.html

East Arrow Park (Maple Cemetery):
http://www.junction.net/vernhist/aarrowpark.html

Edgewood Cemetery:
http://www.junction.net/vernhist/aedgewood.html

Enderby Cliffside Cemetery:
http://www.junction.net/vernhist/aenderbycliff.html

Falkland Cemetery:
http://www.junction.net/vernhist/afalkland.html

Faquier Cemetery:
http://www.junction.net/vernhist/afauquier.html

Grandview Flats Cemetery – Seventh Day Adventist
http://www.junction.net/vernhist/agrandviewflats.html

Grindrod Cemetery – Ukrainian Catholic:
http://www.junction.net/vernhist/agrindrod.html

Hullcar Cemetery: http://www.junction.net/vernhist/ahullcar.html

Lansdowne Cemetery:
http://www.junction.net/vernhist/alansdowne.html

Lumby Cemetery: http://www.junction.net/vernhist/alumby.html

Mara Cemetery: http://www.junction.net/vernhist/amara.html

Monte Creek Cemetery:
http://www.junction.net/vernhist/amontecreek.html

Nakusp
- **Nakusp Cemetery**:
  http://www.junction.net/vernhist/anakusp.html
- **Glenbank Division/Arrow Lake Cemetery**:
  http://www.junction.net/vernhist/anakusp.html

Needles Ferry – Needles Cemetery:
http://www.junction.net/vernhist/aneedles.html

Sicamous Cemetery:
http://www.junction.net/vernhist/asicamous.html

Spallumcheen: St. Ann's Church Cemetery at O'Keefe Ranch
http://www.junction.net/vernhist/aokeefe.html

Trout Lake Cemetery:
http://www.junction.net/vernhist/atrout.html

Vernon Cemetery (Formerly Pioneer Park, Vernon Public Cemetery, Old Pioneer Cemetery, Old Kamloops Road Cemetery): http://www.junction.net/vernhist/avernon.html

Victoria Tombstone Tales of Ross Bay Cemetery / Old Cemeteries Society
http://www.oldcem.bc.ca/
Take a tour of the cemetery or read about some of the 28,000 people buried here.

Westwold

- **Westwold Cemetery (St. Luke's)**: http://www.junction.net/vernhist/awestwold.html
- **Ingram-King Cemetery**: http://www.junction.net/vernhist/aingram-king.html

Winfield Cemetery:
http://www.junction.net/vernhist/awinfield.html

Census Information and Settler Lists

1876 Voters Lists Indexes

- **Cache Creek**: http://www.ocis.net/kfhs/kfhvol11_2.html
- **Clinton**: http://www.ocis.net/kfhs/kfhvol10_1.html
- **Lytton**: http://www.ocis.net/kfhs/kfhvol14_6.html
- **Nicola**: http://www.ocis.net/kfhs/kfhvol12_9.html
- **Yale & Hope**: http://www.ocis.net/kfhs/kfhvol13_3.html

1877 Oblates of Mary Immaculate Census

- http://www.arts.ouc.bc.ca/hist/census/omihome.htm
- **Info/Search**: HTTP://royal.okanagan.bc.ca/census/omi1877.html

Native census conducted by the Oblate Fathers for Head of the Lake, the Okanagan Mission and Spallumcheen. Name, Indian name, sex, age, marital status and "baptismal comments."

1877 Indian Reserve Commission Census

- http://royal.okanagan.bc.ca/cthomson/living_landscapes/census/irc/irchome.html
- **Info/Search**: HTTP://royal.okanagan.bc.ca/census/ind1877.html

25 Indian bands/localities, with English & Indian names, family composition and brief inventory.

1881 Canada Census: Yale District

- http://royal.okanagan.bc.ca/cthomson/living_landscapes/census/1881/1881home.html
- **Info/Search**:
  HTTP://royal.okanagan.bc.ca/census/yale1881.html

Information, by community, includes birthplace, origin, occupation, marital status and age.

1881 Census: Vancouver Island – District 191A: Vancouver South

http://www.geocities.com/Heartland/Acres/5964/81census.htm

Covers the towns of Cedar, Departure Bay, East Wellington, Extension, Harewood, Lantzville, Nanaimo, Nanoose Bay and South Wellington. Includes many Chinese men brought over to work in the coal mines of British Columbia.

1881 Census: Vancouver Island – Subdistrict 190E: Metchosin and Esquimalt

http://www.geocities.com/Heartland/Acres/5964/metesq.htm

Includes the names of Chinese workers brought over to work in the coal mines.

1891 Canada Census: Yale District

- http://royal.okanagan.bc.ca/cthomson/living_landscapes/census/1891/1891home.html
- **Info/Search**:
  HTTP://royal.okanagan.bc.ca/census/yale1891.html

Information includes religion, occupation, age, marital statues and ability to read and write.

Census for British Columbia, District K4 (District 3/F1), "North Nanaimo"
Includes the present-day towns of Nanoose, Parksville, French Creek, Qualicum, Qualicum Bay, Errington, Coombs and Hilliers.
- **1891**: http://macn.bc.ca/~d69hist/1891census.html
- **1901**: http://macn.bc.ca/~d69hist/1901census.html

1901 Census: Union Bay and Courtenay, Including Denman and Hornby Islands
http://www.connected.bc.ca/~genealogy/comox1.html
A transcript of District 3, Sub-district B; Polling Subdivision 1.

1901 Census: Cumberland Town
http://www.connected.bc.ca/~genealogy/comox3.html
A transcript of District 3, Sub-district B; Polling Subdivision 3.

Big Qualicum Settlement – 1901
http://www.geocities.com/Heartland/Acres/5964/qual1901.htm
A list of settlers from Henderson's 1901 BC Gazetteer and Directory.

Chase River Settlers – 1919
http://www.geocities.com/Heartland/Acres/5964/cr1919.htm
A list of settlers, with profession, extracted from Henderson's 1919 Gazetteer and Directory.

Nanoose Bay Settlers – 1919
http://www.geocities.com/Heartland/Acres/5964/nan1919.htm
A list of settlers, with profession, extracted from Henderson's 1919 Gazetteer and Directory.

Salt Spring Island Settlers – 1868
http://web.uvic.ca/history-robinson/settlist.html

Walhachin Voters List Index – 1933
http://www.ocis.net/kfhs/kfhvol11_5.html

Workers Already in Nanaimo in 1854
http://www.geocities.com/Heartland/Acres/5964/workers.htm

Immigration and Passenger Lists

Canadian Border Entry Lists 1908-1918
http://www.cadvision.com/traces/imigrate/cbe.html
A browseable list of surnames ages and point of entry for several border crossings in British Columbia and Dawson, Yukon Territory.

Pioneer Asian Indian Immigration to the Pacific Coast
http://neuheim.ucdavis.edu:80/punjab/
Sections include Why Did They Emigrate?, a map of origins, chronology and historic photos.

Ships Plans Database – Maritime Museum of British Columbia
http://mmbc.bc.ca/searcher/searchplan.html
Search ship plans by name, type, prefix, accession number, date and other criteria.

Ships That Came to Vancouver Island

Passenger lists or a brief description of the ship and the years of service.

- *S.S. Beaver*:
  http://www.geocities.com/Heartland/Acres/5964/ssbeaver.htm
- *Harpooner* (1849):
  http://www.geocities.com/Heartland/Acres/5964/harpoon.htm
- *Cowlitz* (1850):
  http://www.geocities.com/Heartland/Acres/5964/cow.htm
- *Norman Morison* (1850):
  http://www.geocities.com/Heartland/Acres/5964/nmor50.htm
- *Torrie* (1851):
  http://www.geocities.com/Heartland/Acres/5964/torrie.htm
- *Norman Morison* to Victoria (1852):
  http://www.geocities.com/Heartland/Acres/5964/nmor52.htm
- *Norman Morison* to Victoria (1853):
  http://www.geocities.com/Heartland/Acres/5964/nmor53.htm
- *Princess Royal* (1854):
  http://www.geocities.com/Heartland/Acres/5964/princess.htm
- *Princess Royal* (1857):
  http://www.geocities.com/Heartland/Acres/5964/pr1857.htm
- *Princess Royal* (1862):
  http://www.geocities.com/Heartland/Acres/5964/pr1862.htm

Migration and Emigration Data

Ships That Sailed From Victoria

- *Norman Morrison* (to London 1852):
  http://www.geocities.com/Heartland/Acres/5964/nmlon52.htm
- *Norman Morison* (to London 1853):
  http://www.geocities.com/Heartland/Acres/5964/nmor53.htm

Museums/Historic Sites & Groups

Directories

BC Heritage
http://www.heritage.gov.bc.ca/
The official BC government guide to the sites under its jurisdiction in the province. Information on the Heritage Branch and the province-wide BC Heritage Passport.

British Columbia Museums Association Directory and Database
http://www3.islandnet.com/~bcma/
Browse the Directory of Cultural and Natural Heritage by category or city or perform a keyword search in the association's database for museums or communities.

Museums and Historic Sites

Alberni Valley Museum – Port Alberni, BC
http://susan.chin.gc.ca:8016/BASIS/guide/user/search/DDW?M=1&U=1&W=GUIDE_KEY=1267
Exhibits depicting the human and cultural history of the Alberni Valley and West Coast of Vancouver Island, including railway and logging equipment, folk artifacts and crafts.

Barkerville Online – Barkerville, BC
http://cariboo-net.com/sentinel/index.htm
A brief history and virtual tour of this historic town, with over 120 buildings and displays.

BC Forest Museum – Duncan, BC
http://www.bcforestmuseum.com/
Set in a 100-acre park, the museum features displays of artifacts, photographs, buildings and equipment telling the story of the logging industry and forestry in the province.

Boundary Museum – Grand Forks, BC
http://susan.chin.gc.ca:8016/BASIS/guide/user/search/DDW?M=1&U=1&W=GUIDE_KEY=1296
Displays and records of mining, forestry, commerce and agriculture in the Boundary region.

Bulkley Valley Museum – Smithers, BC
http://susan.chin.gc.ca:8016/BASIS/guide/user/search/DDW?M=1&U=1&W=GUIDE_KEY=1344
Info and photos of this museum concentrating on European settlement of the surrounding region.

Carr House – Victoria, BC [English & French]
http://www.tbc.gov.bc.ca/culture/schoolnet/carr/index.htm
A virtual tour, history and biography of Victoria artist and writer Emily Carr.

Chase and District Museum and Archives – Chase, BC
http://susan.chin.gc.ca:8016/BASIS/guide/user/search/DDW?M=1&U=1&W=GUIDE_KEY=1301
Artifacts and archives dealing with the role of farming and logging in the region's development.

Chilliwack Museum and Archives – Chilliwack, BC
http://www.gov.chilliwack.bc.ca/leisure/comm-programs/museum.html
Information and photos on this museum, depicting the history of the District of Chilliwack.

Chilkoot Trail National Historic Site – Dyea, AK to Bennett, BC [English & French]
http://fas.sfu.ca/parkscan/ct/
This 53-km trail was the route to the Klondike during the 1898 Gold Rush.

City of Penticton's R.N. Atkinson Museum and Archives – Penticton, BC
http://susan.chin.gc.ca:8016/BASIS/guide/user/search/DDW?M=1&U=1&W=GUIDE_KEY=1471
Exhibits and historic documents on gold seekers, sternwheelers, railway men and First Nations.

City of White Rock Museum and Archives – White Rock, BC
http://susan.chin.gc.ca:8016/BASIS/guide/user/search/DDW?M=1&U=1&W=GUIDE_KEY=1130
A community museum on the history of White Rock and surrounding towns.

Cottonwood House Historic Site – Quesnel, BC
http://www.heritage.gov.bc.ca/cott/cott.htm
An historic 1860's roadhouse along the infamous Cariboo Wagon Trail.

Courtenay and District Museum: Exhibits – Courtenay, BC
http://www.courtenaymuseum.bc.ca/tour.htm
Information on the First Nations and Pioneer Exhibits, as well as the Archives at this Vancouver Island museum. (Other exhibits include Paleontology – your ancestors aren't *that* old!)

Cowichan Valley Museum – Duncan, BC
http://web.islandnet.com/~bcma/museums/cvm/
Local farming and household equipment, textiles and medical collection from area settler's lives.

Craig Heritage Park and Museum – Parksville, BC
http://www.macn.bc.ca/~d69hist/parkwelc.html
Twelve heritage buildings, including a post office, church, log home, fire hall and school.

Craigdarroch Castle – Victoria, BC
http://www3.islandnet.com/~bcma/museums/cdc/cdc.html
The restored Victorian home of coal industrialist Robert Dunsmuir. Built in 1887-90, the site features stained and leaded glass, woodwork and Victorian furnishings and art.

Craigflower Farm – Victoria, BC
http://www.tbc.gov.bc.ca/culture/schoolnet/craigflower/index.html
Take a virtual tour of this mid-1800's farm, manor and schoolhouse or view the collections.

Cumberland Museum and Archives – Cumberland, BC
http://www.island.net/~cma_chin/
The history of Cumberland, largely focusing on the role of coal mining from 1880 to 1966.

Delta Museum and Archives – Delta, BC
http://www.corp.delta.bc.ca/park&re_museum.htm
Exhibits in a pioneer home depicting early pioneer life, farming, fishing, canning and hunting.

Doukhobor Village Museum – Castlegar, BC
http://www.kootenay.org/doukhobor/museum.html
Displays and recreations of the daily life of these Russian immigrants from Saskatchewan.

Elphinstone Pioneer Museum – Gibsons, BC
http://www.gibsonslibrary.bc.ca/museum/
The regional museum for the Sunshine Coast, from Port Mellon to Egmont, including Gibsons, Roberts Creek, Sechelt and Pender Harbor. Oral histories, photos, newspapers and artifacts.

Fort Langley National Historic Site – Fort Langley, BC [English & French]
http://fas.sfu.ca/parkscan/fl/
Take an online tour or read the history of this restored fort that was "the birthplace of British Columbia," a major fur trading fort and the start of the 1858 Fraser River Gold Rush.

Fort Rodd Hill and Fisgard Lighthouse National Historic Sites – Victoria, BC [English & French]
http://fas.sfu.ca/parkscan/frh/
The history and an online tour of these two sites, the former serving to defend Victoria and the Naval base at Esquimalt Harbor, and the latter the first lighthouse on Canada's west coast.

Fort St. James National Historic Site – Fort St. James, BC [English & French]
http://fas.sfu.ca/parkscan/fsj/
Displays, exhibits and presentations commemorating the fort founded by Simon Fraser in 1806 that served at the headquarters for the fur trade in the district of New Caledonia.

Fort Steele Heritage Town – Fort Steele, BC
http://www.fortsteele.bc.ca/virt.html
A recreated mining boomtown from the 1890's. View over sixty displays, including a tinsmith, blacksmith, farm, eating establishments and performances by costumed interpreters.

Fort Victoria – Victoria, BC
http://www.tbc.gov.bc.ca/culture/schoolnet/fortvic/
Learn about the history, people and fort life at this Hudson's Bay Company post.

Fraser-Fort George Regional Museum – Prince George, BC
http://www.pgonline.com/ffgrm/
Located in the former Hudson's Bay Company fort, this museum presents regional history with interactive multimedia displays. Take a tour of the museum online and view current exhibits.

Greater Vernon Museum and Archives – Vernon, BC
http://susan.chin.gc.ca:8016/BASIS/guide/user/search/DDW?M=1&U=1&W=GUIDE_KEY=949
The history of the region's development presented in an extensive collection of local artifacts.

Gulf of Georgia Cannery National Historic Site – Steveston, BC [English & French]
http://fas.sfu.ca/parkscan/ggc/
Take an online tour of the largest cannery of its kind in the province, or read its history.

Haida Gwaii Museum of Qay'llnagaay – Skidegate, BC
http://susan.chin.gc.ca:8016/BASIS/guide/user/search/DDW?M=1&U=1&W=GUIDE_KEY=1454
The museum, located on the site of the old Haida village of Qay'llnagaay, celebrates the history and culture of the Haida people, as well as the work of present-day artists.

Helmcken House – Victoria, BC
http://www.tbc.gov.bc.ca/culture/schoolnet/helmcken/
Take a virtual tour of the oldest house in Victoria, former home of prominent physician and politician Dr. John Sebastian Helmcken. Collections include his medical equipment and notes.

Historic Hat Creek Ranch – Cache Creek, BC
http://www.heritage.gov.bc.ca/hat/hat.htm
Over 20 historic buildings help bring to life the history of transportation in the region, including the Hudson's Bay Company and Shushwap people's influence in the Bonaparte Valley.

Historic O'Keefe Ranch – Vernon, BC
http://www.okeeferanch.bc.ca/
A collection of several pre-1900 historic buildings, including a log home and barn, mansion, schoolhouse, blacksmith and church. The museum includes displays on ranching and the lifestyle of the interior of the province.

Historic Yale Museum and St. John the Divine Church – Yale, BC
http://www.octonet.com/~prospect/index.html
Learn the history of this Fraser River Gold Rush town at the head of the Cariboo Wagon Road.

Irving House Historic Center and New Westminster Museum/Archives – New Westminster, BC
http://www.city.new-westminster.bc.ca/cityhall/museum/
The Irving House preserves the splendor of a restored Victorian-era home, the Museum houses artifacts from the founding of BC's oldest city in 1859, and the Archives houses historic photographs, files, personal papers, cemetery indexes, etc. for the city and its residents.

Keremeos Grist Mill – Keremeos, BC
- http://www3.islandnet.com/~bcma/museums/gmk/gmk.html
- http://www.heritage.gov.bc.ca/grist/grist.htm

History and visitor information for the mill, built in 1877 on the historic Dewdney Trail.

Kettle Valley Railway Heritage Society – Summerland, BC
http://sage.ark.com/~mcvittie/kvr.htm
"Unofficial" page of this living railway museum operating on a 10 km stretch of the railway.

Kilby Historic Store and Farm – Harrison Mills, BC
http://www.heritage.gov.bc.ca/kilby/kilby.htm
A virtual tour and history of this early 1900's store and the dairy industry in the province.

Kitimat Centennial Museum – Kitimat, BC
http://www.sno.net/kitmuse/
Displays of Haisla culture, the settlement and founding of Kitimat and the aluminum industry.

Kitwanga Fort National Historic Site – between New Hazelton and Terrace, BC [English & French]
http://fas.sfu.ca/parkscan/kf/
Archaeological remains of fortified houses with displays and exhibits celebrating the culture and history of the Tsimshian people, who once used this site as a fort and battleground.

The Maritime Museum of British Columbia – Victoria, BC
http://mmbc.bc.ca/
A clickable map of the museum provides information on the fascinating exhibits depicting the maritime history of the province, including exploration, the development of the shipping trade, BC lighthouses and the online Vintage Vessel Index of historic wooden ships.
The Virtual Maritime Museum [English & French]
http://www.schoolnet.ca/collections/maritime_museum/estart.html
Online exhibits and displays of Adventure (solo circumnavigation), Exploration and Commerce tell the history of the Pacific Northwest. Check out the online Sound Gallery.

McLean Mill National Historic Site – Port Alberni, BC
http://www3.islandnet.com/~bcma/museums/msnhs/msnhs.html
Photos, history and visitor information for this steam-operated sawmill from the 1920's.

Metchosin Schoolhouse and Pioneer Implements Museum – Metchosin, BC
http://www.islandnet.com/~bchap/museum.html
This was the first new schoolhouse opened in BC after confederation.

Museum at Campbell River – Campbell River, BC
http://www.island.net/~crm_chin/
Exhibits, programs and educational tours dedicated to the unique culture and heritage of Northern Vancouver Island. Exhibits include logging, First Nations and outdoor life.

The Museum of Anthropology at the University of British Columbia – Vancouver, BC
http://www.moa.ubc.ca/
Collections and exhibitions celebrating the art and culture of the Northwest Coast First Nations.

Nanaimo District Museum – Nanaimo, BC
- http://www.sd68.nanaimo.bc.ca./nol/community/mus_01.htm
- http://www.island.net/~ndmuseum/

Displays and artifacts reflecting the history and culture of the town and region.

Nelson Museum – Nelson, BC
http://susan.chin.gc.ca:8016/BASIS/guide/user/search/DDW?M=1&U=1&W=GUIDE_KEY=1396
A collection of artifacts from the West Kootenay region and community archives.

North Vancouver Museum and Archives – North Vancouver, BC
http://www.district.north-van.bc.ca/nvma/
Shows the role of logging, shipbuilding, ferries, streetcars, etc. on the culture of the region.

Point Ellice Collection of Household Victoriana – Victoria, BC
[English & French]
http://www.schoolnet.ca/collections/victoriana/
The restored 19th-century home and gardens of Peter and Caroline O'Reilley, with over 4,000 artifacts depicting the lifestyle of the Victorian elite. Take a virtual tour with the houseboy, view objects and clothing by room or read ghost stories and gossip about the family.

Port Hardy Museum and Archives – Port Hardy, BC
http://vogon.capescott.net/~museum/
Online presentations of local Vancouver Island history and photos, plus the museum's gift shop.

Quesnel and District Museum and Archives – Quesnel, BC
http://www.sd28.bc.ca/museum/
Artifacts and archival resources dealing with the early history of the Cariboo region of BC.

Revelstoke Railway Museum – Revelstoke, BC
http://www.revelstokecc.bc.ca/mountns/revrail.htm
Railway equipment and exhibits on the history of "the most treacherous section of terrain on Canada's first transcontinental railway."

Royal British Columbia Museum – Victoria, BC
http://RBCM1.RBCM.GOV.BC.CA/
Go to "collections" to get information about the museum's Human History collections, papers and articles, as well as a link to the Thompson/Okanagan Living Landscapes project.

Saanich Historical Artifacts Society (Heritage Acres) – Saanichton, BC
http://www.horizon.bc.ca/~shas/
Dedicated to preserving memorabilia from BC's pioneer past. Includes a large collection of farm machinery, household artifacts, steam engines, tractors and industrial artifacts.

Salmon Arm Museum and Heritage Association / R.J. Haney Heritage Park and House – Salmon Arm, BC
http://www.sd83.bc.ca/comm/hist/cdnnfmai.htm
A restored house, heritage village and museum depicting the region's economic and cultural past.

Sidney Museum: Marine Mammal and Historical – Sidney, BC
http://www.sidneybc.com/museum/index.htm
Collections include photographs and artifacts of indigenous, European and Oriental people.

Sooke Region Museum – Sooke, (Vancouver Island) BC
http://www.sookenet.com/sooke/museum/
Displays on the logging, trapping, fishing and other lifestyles of Vancouver Island.

Summerland Museum and Historical Society – Summerland, BC
http://susan.chin.gc.ca:8016/BASIS/guide/user/search/DDW?M=1&U=1&W=GUIDE_KEY=1581
Depicting the early growth of the town with authentic displays of pioneer life.

Sunshine Coast Maritime Museum – Gibson's Landing, BC
http://www.sunshine.net/www/1000/sn1095/
Ships' engines, models and charts depicting the maritime heritage of the Sunshine Coast.

U'mista Cultural Center Potlatch Collection – Alert Bay, BC
http://schoolnet2.carleton.ca/english/ext/aboriginal/umista2/index.html
View photos and information on the 160 native masks in the Center's collection.

Valemount and Area Museum – Valemount, BC
http://www.vis.bc.ca/museum.htm
Collections on logging, the railway, pioneer homes and trapper's cabin, area antiques.

Vancouver Maritime Museum – Vancouver, BC
http://www.vmm.bc.ca/
Exhibits focusing on maritime history, art, culture and technology. Includes the RCMP schooner *St. Roch*, Captain George Vancouver's charting equipment and many scale models of ships.

Vancouver Police Department Police Museum – Vancouver, BC
http://www.city.vancouver.bc.ca/police/museum/
The museum invites you to "Discover mystery, history and intrigue."

Wells, BC
http://cariboo-net.com/sentinel/wells.htm
A description and visitor information for this re-created 1930's mining town.

West Coat Railway Association Heritage Park – Squamish, BC
http://www.wcra.org/heritage/index.htm
A collection of 62 pieces of heritage railway "rolling stock" and railway related artifacts representing the major railways that have served British Columbia.

Xats'ull Heritage Village – near William's Lake, BC
http://www.cariboo-net.com/xatsull.html
Experience the traditional Shuswap lifestyle amid pit houses and teepees while you learn about the old ways, crafts, skills and traditions of the aboriginal people of the Cariboo region.

Professional Organization

British Columbia Museums Association
http://www3.islandnet.com/~bcma/museums/bcma/index.html
A professional organization providing advocacy, training, publications, technical assistance, conferences and other means of support for institutions and museum staff in the province.

Military, Native and Historic Groups

Military Heritage Society of British Columbia
http://www.clearcf.uvic.ca/bcmhs/
Information on the group, a sample of the newsletter, upcoming events and a merchandise page.

South Island Métis Nation – Victoria, BC
http://www.get-info.net/metis/
Basic contact information for the group, along with its mission statement.

Tribes and Bands of British Columbia
http://hanksville.phast.umass.edu:8000/cultprop/contacts/tribal/BC.html
A list of native groups in the province, with contact information and links, where available.

Provincial and Local History and Photos

Provincial and Regional History and Photos

BC Studies
http://www.interchg.ubc.ca/bcstudie/
A quarterly publication dedicated to the culture and traditions of the province. Browse the tables of contents for recent issues or an index to regular and special issues.

A Brief History of the Comox Valley
http://www.bctravel.com/ni/comoxhis.html

The British Columbia Archives Presents the Amazing Time Machine
http://www.bcarchives.gov.bc.ca/exhibits/timemach/index.htm
A great site for kids and teachers to have access to and learn about provincial history.

British Columbia Geographical Names
http://www.env.gov.bc.ca/gdbc/placenames/
Search place names, get correct spelling and exact location, plus other information.

Captain Alejandro Malaspina
http://www.mala.bc.ca/www/discover/capt/capt.htm
A brief introduction to this Spanish-born explorer of the Pacific Coast.

Early British Columbia Surveying History
http://www.env.gov.bc.ca/srmb/survhist.htm
Photos and explanatory descriptions of early efforts to geographically document the province.

The First Newspapers on Canada's West Coast: 1858-1863
http://members.tripod.com/~Hughdoherty/index.htm
A history of journalism, originally presented as a graduate thesis at the University of Victoria. Illustrated with images from the BC Archives.

Fragmentary Evidence of Spanish "Invasion"
http://ogopogo.com/okanagan/spanish/index.html
An article exploring the possibility of early Spanish presence in the Okanagan Valley.

GeoData BC Newsletter Index
http://www.env.gov.bc.ca/srmb/news/newsindx.htm
Each newsletter includes an article on the origin/history of a geographic location in BC.

George Vancouver: "A Chart Shewing Part of the Coast of N.W. America"
http://www.lib.virginia.edu/exhibits/lewis_clark/ch4-26.html
A chart and explanation from Vancouver's 1798 book *A Voyage of discovery to the North Pacific ocean, and Round the World.*

A History of the Northwest Coast
http://www.hallman.org/indian/.www.html
An historical timeline, with links to images and text on natives and European settlers.

Kettle Valley Railway Homepage'
http://www.interlog.com/~hturner/KVRsite/KVRhome.html
A comprehensive history, with first-hand accounts and photos, of this stretch of railway.

Living Landscapes: Historic Photographs
HTTP://royal.okanagan.bc.ca/histphoto/index.html
A searchable collection of photos from the Thompson/Okanagan region of the province.

Moving Image Collections: BC Archives
http://www.bcarchives.gov.bc.ca/exhibits/movies/movimage.htm
Download MPEG videos of various events from recent British Columbia history.

***Okanagan History* Index**
http://royal.okanagan.bc.ca/info/ohs.html
A searchable index to *Okanagan History: Reports of the Okanagan Historical Society.*

Onderdonk's Way: Building the Canadian Pacific Railway in British Columbia
http://www.galleries.bc.ca/kamloops/onderdonk.html
A virtual exhibition from the Kamloops Art Gallery. Historical photos, essays and maps.

Simon Fraser, The Explorer
http://www.sfu.ca/archives/sf-explorer.html
A brief biographical sketch of the explorer of "New Caledonia" and other parts of BC.

South Vancouver Island Communities
http://www.cvvm.com/vm-comm.html
Links to brief historic and current information about the towns in this region.

University of British Columbia Historic Photographs Database
http://www.library.ubc.ca/spcoll/ubc_arch/photos.html
A searchable database of about 26,000 of the collection of 200,000 photos at the library.

Cultural Groups

The Canadian Ethnic Chinese Contribution to British Columbia
http://rbcm1.rbcm.gov.bc.ca/discover/ds24195/4canmos.html
An essay on the economic and cultural impact of Chinese-Canadians in the early province.

The French Presence in Canada and in British Columbia
http://www.corp.direct.ca/news/french/french1.shtml
An overview of the achievements and contributions of the Francophone population, with emphasis on its origins and development in British Columbia.

History of Blacks in British Columbia
http://www.islandnet.com/~bcbhas/history.htm
Articles, including The Arrival of Blacks in BC and biographies of prominent individuals.

Local History and Photos

Alert Bay History
http://www.alertbay.com/brief.htm

Bridge River-Lillooet Country
http://members.home.net/ironmtn/lillooet.html
Photos, history and legends about this area of the province.

Campbell River – A Brief History of the Campbell River Area
http://www.bctravel.com/ni/camphist.html

Chilliwack – History of the District of Chilliwack
http://www.gov.chilliwack.bc.ca/tourism/history/
A brief look at the development of the town and district, with historic photos.

Chemainus – Town of Chemainus
http://www.cowichan.bc.ca/places/chemain.html
Includes an overview of the town's history and development.

Columbia/Shuswap Area History
http://www.shuswap.bc.ca/sunny/ed-hist.htm
A brief overview, including discovery, steamboat navigation, mining and logging.

Colwood Firefighters Historical Society
http://www.vicsurf.com/cvfd/history.htm
Actually the history of the Colwood Volunteer Fire Department 1940's-1980's.

Duncan – A Brief History of Duncan and the Cowichan Valley
http://www.bctravel.com/si/dunchist1.html

Esquimalt History
http://www.mun.esquimalt.bc.ca/Administration/esq-adm/history.html#top
Origin of the name, native and European settlers, agriculture, Royal Navy and development.

Fort Langley – A Brief History of Fort Langley
http://users.uniserve.com/~gborden/fl-hist.htm

Fort St. John: The Changing Faces of the North Peace [English/French]
http://www.schoolnet.ca/collections/north_peace/
An online exhibit of some 200 photographs and descriptive text chronicling the evolution of this town and region in the areas of Transportation, Women Pioneers, Economy, Industry, Interesting People and Early Forts.

Gang Ranch Chronology
http://members.home.net/ironmtn/lillooet.html

Gulf of Georgia Cannery History
http://www.canfisco.com/gs-gulf.html
An illustrated history of this important economic and industrial center.

Ladysmith: The Naming of a Town
http://www.geocities.com/Heartland/Acres/5964/lady.htm

Metchosin
- **History**: http://www.islandnet.com/~bchap/methist.html
- **Pioneers**: http://www.islandnet.com/~bchap/metpion.html

Nelson – History of the City of Nelson
http://www.city.nelson.bc.ca/html/history.html
Includes information on the city's founding, plus a "virtual motoring tour" of the city and a "virtual walking tour" of the downtown core.

North Vancouver's Industrial History

- **Industrial Landscape**: http://www3.islandnet.com/~bcma/museums/ihg/ihg1.html
- **Jobs**: http://www3.islandnet.com/~bcma/museums/ihg/ihg2.html
- **People**: http://www3.islandnet.com/~bcma/museums/ihg/ihg3.html

Osoyoos – The History of Osoyoos
http://www.town.osoyoos.bc.ca/b/history.html

Parksville – History of Parksville
http://www.macn.bc.ca/~d69hist/history.html
A timeline of the town from 1792 through 1991, showing highlights of Parksville history.

Parksville/Qualicum Beach – A Brief History of Parksville and the Qualicam Beach Area
http://www.bctravel.com/ci/pqhist.html

Port Hardy History
http://www.capescott.net/dphardy/basic/history.html
An overview of the development of this small harbor town since the turn of the century.

Prince George – A Short History of Prince George
http://vortex.netbistro.com/bistro/pg/history.shtml

Quesnelle Forks and Likely
http://www.cariboo-net.com/sentinel/qforks.htm
A brief history of the "ghost town" of Quesnelle Forks and the nearby town of Likely.

Richmond Facts: Brief History
http://www.city.richmond.bc.ca/facts/facts.htm#History

Richmond Facts: Brief History
http://www.city.richmond.bc.ca/facts/facts.htm#History
An overview of the city's history from pre-contact through industrial development to today.

Richmond – History of Richmond Municipality
http://www.city.richmond.bc.ca/archives/ex_thom/mtexiba.html
A virtual exhibit of the full 1923 text written by Mary Thompson, complete with all 40 images.

(Salt Spring Island) Who Killed William Robinson?
An illustrated true mystery, showing the complex relations between Black and Aboriginal people in this tiny community in the late 1860's.

Sidney – History of Sidney
http://www.sidneybc.com/museum/hst_sdny.htm
An overview of the municipality, from the early Saanich people to fur trading and exploration.

Surrey – History of Surrey
http://www.city.surrey.bc.ca/about/history.html
From its origins as a native settlement to its development as the second largest city in BC.

Union – Trent River Train Disaster
http://www.geocities.com/Heartland/Acres/5964/trent.htm
An article from the Victoria *Daily Colonist* from 18 August 1898. Lists the fatalities and injured.

Vancouver – A Brief History of Vancouver
http://www.city.vancouver.bc.ca/ctyclerk/aboutvan.html
An overview of the city's history, presented as an historical timeline with highlights.

Links to Your Canadian Past
Ontario and the Western Provinces

Vancouver – Discover Vancouver: Local History
http://www.discovervancouver.com/history/history_index.shtml
Essays and a chronology of local history from "The Greater Vancouver Book."

Vancouver – The Great Depression in Vancouver
http://www2.excite.sfu.ca/pgm/depress/greatdepress.html
A comprehensive historical project developed by students at the Point Grey Mini School.

Victoria – History of Victoria
http://www.city.victoria.bc.ca/history.htm
Historic overview of the city, with information on several historic buildings.

Victoria, British Columbia, 1889
http://www.bcarchives.gov.bc.ca/exhibits/birdseye/victoria.htm
An overview engraving of the city, with a list of local buildings. Clicking on a building name takes you to a corresponding list of visual records located at the BC Archives, all viewable.

Victoria – The Port of Victoria [English & French]
http://www.schoolnet.ca/collections/maritime_museum/commerce/portvic.html
Click on several locations in this 1878 map of Victoria Harbor for images and explanation of historical people, events and structures associated with that particular site.

Yale: http://www.octonet.com/~prospect/overview.html

- **Fraser River Gold Rush**:
  http://www.octonet.com/~prospect/frasergold.html
- **Canadian Pacific Railway**:
  http://www.octonet.com/~prospect/cpr.html
- **Cariboo Wagon Road**:
  http://www.octonet.com/~prospect/cariboo.html
- **St. John the Divine Church**:
  http://www.octonet.com/~prospect/church.html

Family Associations/Surnames

Province-wide and Regional Surnames

Abbotsford Genealogy Group Surname Interests
http://www3.bc.sympatico.ca/abbotsfordgengroup/AGG.HTML#SURNAME

BC GenWeb Queries
http://www.islandnet.com/cgi-bin/postit?login=jveinot&topic=/genweb/bcqueries
Browse by keyword, author, date or subject. You can also post a new query via this site.

British Columbia Genealogical Society Surname Queries
http://www.npsnet.com/bcgs/querypag.htm
A list of both member and non-member queries regarding the surnames of families from British Columbia. Non-member queries are accepted for a small fee.

Campbell River Genealogy Club Surname Interests

- **A-D**: http://www.connected.bc.ca/~genealogy/a-d.html
- **E-H**: http://www.connected.bc.ca/~genealogy/e-h.html
- **I-L**: http://www.connected.bc.ca/~genealogy/i-l.html
- **M, Mc, Mac**: http://www.connected.bc.ca/~genealogy/m.html
- **N-P**: http://www.connected.bc.ca/~genealogy/n-p.html
- **Q-T**: http://www.connected.bc.ca/~genealogy/q-t.html
- **U-Z**: http://www.connected.bc.ca/~genealogy/u-z.html

Kamloops Family History Society Surname Interests
http://www.ocis.net/kfhs/kfhist93a.html

Kelowna and District Genealogical Society Surname Index
http://www.wkpowerlink.com/~gjespers/surname.htm

Queries for British Columbia – Canadian Genealogy Made Easy
http://www.geocities.com/Heartland/4051/bcq.htm
View recent queries or submit your own via an online form.

Richmond Archives Biography Files
http://www.city.richmond.bc.ca/archives/biofiles.html
Index to the files on notable families and individuals, including pioneers and longtime residents.

Salt Spring Island Biographies
http://web.uvic.ca/history-robinson/bio.html
Short stories and sketches of early settlers of Salt Spring Island.

Sidney Pioneer Families
http://www.sidneybc.com/museum/hst_pion.htm
Brief biographies and photos of early pioneers to the town and surrounding area.

South Cariboo Genealogy Group Member Interests
http://www.web-trek.net/stern/membinfo.html

Thompson/Okanagan Living Landscapes Biography Projects
HTTP://royal.okanagan.bc.ca/cgi-bin/findproject?biogr
Includes information on the projects Autobiographical Writing of the BC Interior, Dictionary of Okanagan Biography, The Women of O'Keefe Ranch and individual biographies.

Vernon and District Family History Society Surname Interests
http://www.junction.net/vernhist/V5.html

Individual Surnames and Family Associations

Bidewell: http://www.familytreemaker.com/users/b/i/d/William-H-Bidewell/index.html

Binley: http://www.familytreemaker.com/users/e/d/g/James-S-Edgar/ODT2-0001.html

Carlow: http://www3.bc.sympatico.ca/PATSY/

Craig: http://www.familytreemaker.com/users/e/d/g/James-S-Edgar/ODT4-0001.html

Helmcken:
http://www.tbc.gov.bc.ca/culture/schoolnet/helmcken/people/index.html

Hendy:
http://www.stardate.bc.ca/pmhendy/pam/d0000/g0000005.htm#I044

Irvine: http://www.islandnet.com/~wji/ifgginfo.html

Jesperson:
http://www.geocities.com/Heartland/Hills/3730/pedigree.html

McCormick: http://www.mccormickfamily.com/

Minckler: http://www.kent.net/~ilmeyer/thoresen.html#Minckler

Peppan/Peppin/Pepin: http://www.escargot.com/lisap/

Thoresen: http://www.kent.net/~ilmeyer/genealogy.html

Steptoe: http://www.familytreemaker.com/users/r/o/b/Eileen-M-Robinson/index.html

Chat Rooms and Mailing Lists

British Columbia Mailing List:
majordomo@listserv.northwest.com
all: subscribe british-columbia;
digest: subscribe british-columbia-digest

Manitoba

Genealogical, Historical and Cultural Societies

Centre Culturel Franco-Manitobain [French only]
http://francoculture.ca/ccfm/index.html
Dedicated to promoting francophone culture in the province of Manitoba as well as increasing awareness of Franco-Manitoban culture outside the province. Activities include participation in music, literary and art festivals, exhibitions and special activities.

East European Genealogical Society
http://www.eegsociety.org/
Identifies and collects resources pertaining to all countries, religions and ethnic groups of Eastern Europe. Publishes the *East European Genealogist*, with a list of back issues and articles online.

Genealogical Institute of the Jewish Historical Society of Western Canada
http://www.concentric.net/~Lkessler/geninst.shtml
Includes "An Introduction to Jewish Genealogy in Manitoba" and J-GEMS, the Jewish Genealogical Exploration Guide for Manitoba and Saskatchewan.

Icelandic National League of North America: Manitoba Chapters
http://users.imag.net/~sry.rasgeirs/INL-NewsEventsMan.html
Links to contacts and news of the Brúin, Selkirk Chapter; Esjan, Arborg Chapter; Fálkinn, Brandon Chapter; Gimli Chapter and Icelandic Canadian Frón Lundar Chapter of the INL

Links to Your Canadian Past

Ontario and the Western Provinces

The Jewish Historical Society of Western Canada
http://www.concentric.net/~Lkessler/jhswc.shtml
Dedicated to recording the history and culture of the Jewish people of the Canadian West. Maintains archives, lectures, an oral history program, a newsletter and other projects.

Manitoba Genealogical Society
http://www.winnipeg.freenet.mb.ca/mangens/
Information on the quarterly journal *Generations*, hours and holdings of the Resource Center, research requests and projects, including the society's extensive index of cemetery transcriptions.

Manitoba Mennonite Historical Society
http://www.mmhs.org/

Manitoba Multicultural Resource Centre, Inc.
http://www.winnipeg.freenet.mb.ca/mmrc/
Dedicated to promoting and preserving the rich multicultural heritage of the province.

Manitoba GenWeb Project
http://www.rootsweb.com/~canmb/index.htm
Links to genealogical information and resources, indexed in the sections below.

Military History Society of Manitoba – Winnipeg, MB
http://www.gatewest.net/~gcros/
Dedicated to preserving and perpetuating the military history of the province. The society maintains a library with archives, photographs and a small collection of artifacts.

Société Historique de Saint-Boniface (Winnipeg) [English & French]
http://home.ican.net/~shsb/
A wealth of information on the French presence in Manitoba. Includes chronological histories of French Manitoba and the diocese of Saint-Boniface, histories and genealogies of local families, a list and description of items in their archives, and a genealogical research request form.

Professional Organizations

Community Heritage Manitoba
http://www.angelfire.com/biz/CHM/index.html
An umbrella organization for Municipal Heritage Advisory Committees throughout the province, seeking to exchange information, provide education, promote heritage and promote partnerships.

Manitoba Heritage Federation, Inc.
http://www.mts.net/~mhf/
Advocates financial, educational and popular support for the identification, preservation and promotion of all aspects of heritage in the province. Maintains the Manitoba Heritage Library.

Archives

Archive Centers

Boissevain Community Archives
http://www.town.boissevain.mb.ca/archives/
Local histories and genealogies, census and cemetery records and a wealth of other material on the town of Boissevain and surrounding communities. Resources are searchable online.

Department of Archives and Special Collections – University of Manitoba Libraries
http://www.umanitoba.ca/academic_support/libraries/units/archives/
Includes the Archives of the Agricultural Experience, searchable archives of the *Winnipeg Tribune*, an Audio-Visual collection and other holdings. A searchable guide is available.

Mennonite Heritage Centre
http://www.mbnet.mb.ca/~mhc/
The archives holds the records of the Conference of Mennonites in Canada, MCC (Canada), Canadian Mennonite Board of Colonization, Evangelical Mennonites Mission Conference, Prussian and Russian Mennonite community documents, etc., and many personal papers.

Provincial Archives of Manitoba
http://www.gov.mb.ca/chc/archives/
Includes a searchable version of the Access and Privacy Directory, whereby the public can have access to government records under the Freedom of Information and Protection of Privacy Act.

Transcona Historical Museum Archives – Winnipeg, MB
http://members.xoom.com/Transcona/archives.htm
A description of the collections relating to local government and organizations and the railroad. Objects in the museum's collections are searchable online.

United Church of Canada – Manitoba and Northwestern Ontario Conference Archives
http://www.uccan.org/archives/manitoba.htm
Contains records of the Methodist, Presbyterian and Congregational Churches in the conference before 1925 and records of the United Church of Canada after 1925.

Professional Association

Association of Manitoba Archives [English & French]
http://www.pangea.ca/~ama/
A professional organization providing training and education, advocacy, advisory services and grants to those working to preserve Manitoba's archival heritage.

Libraries and Resource Centers

Directories and Catalogs

HYTELNET Library Catalogues – Manitoba
http://moondog.usask.ca/hytelnet/ca0/MB.html
Links to library catalogues in the province that are searchable via telnet, with instructions.

Library Web sites and Catalogues: Manitoba
http://www.nlc-bnc.ca/canlib/emani.htm
An alphabetical listing of public, private and university library Web sites and/or catalogues.

Public Library Services Web Access to MAPLIN
http://pls.chc.gov.mb.ca:8080/z3950/zform.cgi
Access to MAPLIN, the provincial union catalogue for Manitoba public libraries, containing approximately 360,000 titles representing about 720,000 books.

Libraries and Research Centers

Centre for Mennonite Brethren Studies
http://www.cdnmbconf.ca/mb/cmbs.htm
Collects and preserves historical and genealogical records pertaining to the Mennonite community. A guide to the archival holdings, including personal papers, is available.

Centre for Rupert's Land Studies – University of Winnipeg
http://www.uwinnipeg.ca/academic/ic/rupert/index.html
Facilitates scholarly research and publications concerning the former Hudson's Bay Company territory. Publishes the *Rupert's Land Newsletter*, with article excerpts online.

Manitoba Legislative Library – Special Manitoba Heritage Collections
http://www.gov.mb.ca/leg-lib/webmb.html#webmb
Contains the most extensive collection of Manitoba newspapers published since 1859 as well as a collection of Manitoba community and family histories.

Birth, Marriage, Death, Census and Other Data Online

Vital Statistics and Parish Records

Manitoba Vital Statistics Office
http://www.gov.mb.ca/cca/vital.html
Official information on where to write or call to obtain birth, marriage, death and other info.

Manitoba Vital Records
http://www.familytreemaker.com/00000156.html
Contact info for obtaining vital records, with a brief description of records available.

Consolidated Index of the Bergthaler/Chortitzer Church Family Registers
http://www.mbnet.mb.ca/~mhc/allindxm.htm
Marriage index for the following Mennonite churches: Bergthaler (Russia) 1843 and Chortitzer (Manitoba) 1878, 1887, 1907. Listed by husband or wife's surname. Scroll sideways for info.

Composite Index of Early Manitoba Mennonite Church Records
http://www.mmhs.org/canada/super/super.htm
Index of the heads of household for the Bergthal Gemeinde, Chortitzer Gemeinde, Reinlaender Gemeinde, Sommerfelder Gemeinde and Kleine Gemeinde.

Index to the Reinlaender Mennonite Church Register
http://www.mmhs.org/canada/reinland.htm
Includes an informative introduction and key to reading the index.

Sommerfield Gemeinde Buch Cumulative Index
http://www.mmhs.org/canada/sommerf.htm
Index of volumes 1-5 of this Mennonite branch, listed by husband's surname.

Census and Settler Lists

Owen Keveney's Party – 1812
http://members.tripod.com/~tmsnyder/OWEN.htm
Men who enlisted from Mull, Broan and Sligo and went to the York Factory and Red River.

Red River Settlers 1815 – Duncan Cameron's Party
http://members.tripod.com/~tmsnyder/RED.htm
List of settlers who arrived at Holland River 6 September 1815.

Red River Settlement – 1827 Census
http://www.televar.com/~gmorin/27rrs.htm
From the Hudson's Bay Company archives. Includes European and Métis settlers.

Selkirk and Coy Settlers
http://members.tripod.com/~tmsnyder/ROSS.htm
Settlers and servants who enlisted from Ross, Brolas and Greenburn (Island of Mull) for the Honourable H.B. Coy and the Earl of Selkirk.

York Factory Names of 1811
http://members.tripod.com/~tmsnyder/PWL.htm
Men who arrived at Hudson Bay in 1811 and left the York Factory for the interior in 1812.

Immigration and Passenger Lists

Prince of Wales Immigration List 1813
http://members.tripod.com/~tmsnyder/PW_LIST.htm
List of passengers who emigrated from Scotland to the York Factory aboard this vessel.

Prince of Wales Immigration List 1815
http://members.tripod.com/~tmsnyder/PWALES.htm
Mostly immigrants from Old Kildonan to the York Factory and Red River settlement.

Museums & Historic Sites/Groups

Museums and Historic Sites

Boissevain – Online Walking Tour of Heritage Buildings
http://www.town.boissevain.mb.ca/heritage/tour/index.htm
Take a cyber-stroll past some of the historic buildings built by early settlers, including St. Paul's and St. Matthew's Churches, the Agriculture and Land Titles Offices and several historic homes.

Camp Hughes Provincial Historical Site – near Carberry, MB
http://www.gatewest.net/~gcros/cmphghes.html
History and photos of this training camp for the Canadian Expeditionary Force in World War I.

Captain Kennedy Tea House and Museum – St. Andrews, MB
http://susan.chin.gc.ca:8016/BASIS/guide/user/serch/DDW?M=1&U=1&W=GUIDE_KEY=1330
The original 1866 home of Capt. William Kennedy, typical of the Red River Settlement.

Carberry Plains Museum – Carberry, MB
http://susan.chin.gc.ca:8016/BASIS/guide/user/search/DDW?M=1&U=1&W=GUIDE_KEY=751
A local history museum with many artifacts and displays of European homesteaders 1878-1950.

Chapman Museum – Brandon, MB
http://susan.chin.gc.ca:8016/BASIS/guide/user/search/DDW?M=1&U=1&W=GUIDE_KEY=1308
A recreated historic village with 16 buildings, including a school, church, pioneer homes & railroad station.

Dalnavert Museum – Winnipeg, MB
http://www.mhs.mb.ca/museums/dalnavhp.htm
The restored 1895 home of Premier Sir Hugh John MacDonald. A typical Queen Anne-style home which reflects the way the Victorian upper class lived in Manitoba.

Daly House Museum
http://netmaster.docker.com/~taylord/dalyhouse/dalyhouse.html
Take a walk through this house as it must have appeared in the 1880's and 1890's, complete with furniture, wallpaper, decorations and more.

Darlingford School Heritage Museum – Darlingford, MB
http://susan.chin.gc.ca:8016/BASIS/guide/user/search/DDW?M=1&U=1&W=GUIDE_KEY=1324
A restored 1910 brick schoolhouse with artifacts from local daily life from settlement to today.

Dufferin Historical Museum – Carman, MB
http://susan.chin.gc.ca:8016/BASIS/guide/user/search/DDW?M=1&U=1&W=GUIDE_KEY=1323
Displays of pioneer artifacts on local history and agriculture, including photos, toys, clothing.

Dugald Costume Museum – Dugald, MB
http://www.dugaldcostumemuseum.mb.ca/
A collection of over 35,000 men's, women's and children's clothing and textiles from 1700 to the present. Also contains an archive of over 4,000 photographs for researchers.

First Ukrainian Church in Canada – near Gardenton, MB
http://www.infoukes.com/culture/architecture/first_church/
Information and historic photos of St. Michael's Ukrainian Orthodox Church, built in 1899.

The Forks National Historic Site – Winnipeg, MB [English & French]
http://parkscanada.pch.gc.ca/parks/manitoba/the_forks/the_forkse.htm
Much information on the history of this site, the present-day activities and exhibits commemorating this trade, immigration and transportation hub. Online tour available.

Fort Dauphin Museum, Inc. – Dauphin, MB
http://susan.chin.gc.ca:8016/BASIS/guide/user/search/DDW?M=1&U=1&W=GUIDE_KEY=1318
Pioneer buildings and artifacts from the fur trade and settlement eras, surrounded by the palisade of an 18th century fur trading post. Also an archaeological resource center and archive.

Fort La Reine Museum and Pioneer Village – Portage la Prairie, MB
http://susan.chin.gc.ca:8016/BASIS/guide/user/search/DDW?M=1&U=1&W=GUIDE_KEY=1328
Includes a replica of La Vérendrye's Fort La Reine, an 1879 log cabin, pioneer church and school, blacksmith shop, trading post, trapper's cabin and other recreated buildings and displays.

Heritage North Museum and Archives– Thompson, MB
http://www.mysterynet.mb.ca/museum/index.html
Two log cabins with displays on mining, fur trading and natural and pioneer history.

Lower Fort Garry National Historic Site – Selkirk, MB
[English & French]
http://parkscanada.pch.gc.ca/parks/manitoba/lower_fort_garry/lower_fort_garrye.htm
Information, history, photos and an online guided tour of this 19th century fur trading post, where costumed interpreters enact scenes from the daily life of this Hudson's Bay Company fort.

Manitoba Agricultural Museum – Austin, MB
http://www.cyberspc.mb.ca/~a1comptr/agricult.htm
Displays of farming memorabilia and operational agricultural equipment of the pioneer era.

Manitoba Crafts Museum and Library – Winnipeg, MB
http://susan.chin.gc.ca:8016/BASIS/guide/user/search/DDW?M=1&U=1&W=GUIDE_KEY=1390
Displays and documentation on handmade local crafts from historical times to the present day.

Manitoba Museum of Man and Nature – Winnipeg, MB
http://www.manitobamuseum.mb.ca/
Includes the Ethnology collection on native peoples, the Human History Collection, presenting provincial history from settlement to today and the Hudson's Bay Company Collection.

Mennonite Heritage Village – Steinbach, Manitoba
http://www.mts.net/~pklassen/
A re-created historic Mennonite village, with school, houses, church, granary and much more.

Naval Museum of Manitoba – Winnipeg, MB
http://www.naval-museum.mb.ca/
A history of the Manitobans who served in the Canadian navy and the ships on which they served, as well as ships named after locales in the province. Many photos and articles.

Prince of Wales Fort National Historic Site – Churchill, MB
[English & French]
http://parkscanada.pch.gc.ca/parks/manitoba/Prince_Wales_Fort/Prince_Wales_Forte.htm
Information on this site, linked with the Parks Canada Visitors Centre in Churchill, the Norway House, Cape Merry and Sloop's Cove.

Riel House National Historic Site – St. Vital (Winnipeg), MB
http://parkscanada.pch.gc.ca/parks/manitoba/riel_house/riel_housee.htm
Home of the Métis leader and his family. This Web site provides information on the history of Riel and the Métis as well as the site, including an online guided tour.

Saint Andrew's Rectory National Historic Site – Selkirk, MB
[English & French]
http://parkscanada.pch.gc.ca/parks/manitoba/st_andrews_rectory/st_andrews_rectorye.htm
An example of 19th century Red River architecture, housing exhibits on regional architecture and the roles of the Church Missionary Society and Church of England in the West.

Satterthwaite Heritage Log Cabin (McCreary Heritage Advisory Committee) – McCreary, MB
http://susan.chin.gc.ca:8016/BASIS/guide/user/search/DDW?M=1&U=1&W=GUIDE_KEY=1315
A restored log cabin, one-room school house, pioneer heritage garden and period artifacts on the Burrows Trail. Displays of constructing log cabins.

Swan Valley Museum – Swan River, MB
http://susan.chin.gc.ca:8016/BASIS/guide/user/search/DDW?M=1&U=1&W=GUIDE_KEY=1316
The 15 historic buildings include churches, a country store, school, blacksmith shop, railroad station, bake oven and telephone office. Displays feature agricultural and household equipment.

Transcona Historical Museum – Winnipeg, MB
http://members.xoom.com/Transcona/
Includes displays of artifacts relating to local daily and work life, clothing and textiles, the railroad, rare books, photographs and local history archives.

Trembowla Cross of Freedom Inc. Museum – Rural Municipality of Dauphin, MB
http://susan.chin.gc.ca:8016/BASIS/guide/user/search/DDW?M=1&U=1&W=GUIDE_KEY=1314
Includes the first Ukrainian Catholic Church in Canada (with records dating 1920-1960), a replica of a pioneer home and the Trembowla School (with records dating back to 1919).

A Short Pictorial History on Upper Fort Garry – Winnipeg, MB
http://www.mbnet.mb.ca/~botan/history.html
A brief history of "the most important fort in the development of Western Canada." Includes a text overview of the fort's history, plus photos and maps of the fort.

Waskada Museum – Waskada, MB
http://susan.chin.gc.ca:8016/BASIS/guide/user/search/DDW?M=1&U=1&W=GUIDE_KEY=1628
A collection of local household and farming artifacts and machinery, as well as newspapers, ledgers, family bibles and photographs, etc. from the late 1800's and early 1900's.

Wasyl Negrych Pioneer Homestead – Rural Municipality of Gilbert Plains, MB
http://susan.chin.gc.ca:8016/BASIS/guide/user/search/DDW?M=1&U=1&W=GUIDE_KEY=1379
Log cabins and artifacts relating to Ukrainian settlement, including a 100-year-old homestead.

Watson Crossley Community Museum – Grandview, MB
http://susan.chin.gc.ca:8016/BASIS/guide/user/search/DDW?M=1&U=1&W=GUIDE_KEY=1321
Eight restored buildings, including an 1896 pioneer homestead, 1918 3-storey home, rural schoolhouse, Ukrainian Orthodox Church and main museum building with exhibits.

Winnipeg Police Museum
http://www.city.winnipeg.mb.ca/police/history/museum.html
Exhibits include uniforms, equipment, vehicles, original "wanted" posters and a holding cell.

York Factory National Historic Site – Churchill, MB [English & French]
http://parkscanada.pch.gc.ca/parks/manitoba/york_factory/york_factorye.htm
Information on this historic site of the Hudson's Bay Company and fur trade in the 1800's.

Military, Native and Historic Groups

Fort Garry Horse Regimental Home Page
http://www.escape.ca/~fgh/
Includes historical information on this unit of the 38th Canadian Brigade Group.

Tribes and Bands of Manitoba
http://hanksville.phast.umass.edu:8000/cultprop/contacts/tribal/Man.html
A list of the various tribal groups in the province, with contact information and/or links.

United Empire Loyalists Association of Canada – Manitoba Branch
http://home.cc.umanitoba.ca/~umluther/uelac_manitoba/
Membership & activity info, plus a list of members' loyalist ancestors.

Provincial and Local History and Photos

Provincial and Cultural History

Hutterite Place Names in North America: 101 Schmeideleut Colonies (1973)
http://feefhs.org/hut/h-splace.html
Includes many Hutterite communities in Manitoba, with year of founding.

The Voyage to Gimli: Icelandic Emigration to Manitoba
http://nyherji.is/~halfdan/westward/willowp.htm
An article on the arrival of Icelandic settlers in Manitoba, an abbreviation from the *Gimli Saga.*

The Western Canada Pictorial Index, Inc.
http://www.winnipeg.freenet.mb.ca/wcpi/
Information on this collection of over 60,000 images relating to the history of Western Canada.

Local History and Photos

Fisher Branch History
http://www.evergreen.freenet.mb.ca/fisherbranch/history.html
A detailed and informative three-page history of the settlement of the town by French and Ukrainian pioneers and its subsequent development, accompanied by photographs.

Portage la Prairie History
http://www.cpnet.net/portage/city/history.html
A brief overview of the city's history, with a list of historic facts.

Thompson and Area Historic Photos
http://www.mysterynet.mb.ca/museum/archives/archives.htm
From the Heritage North Museum and archives, historical pictures of the growth and development of Thompson, plus many unidentified photos the museum needs your help with.

Winnipeg: Our Colourful Past
http://WWW.Tourism.Winnipeg.MB.CA/Intr_TT.htm
Includes an overview of fur trade and settlement, Jean-Baptiste Lagimodière, the Riel Rebellion, "Chicago of the North" and Winnipeg Today.

Family Associations/Surnames

Manitoba GenWeb Surname Index
http://cgi.rootsweb.com/surhelp-bin/surindx.pl?gc=/Canada/Manitoba/General
A searchable index of surnames submitted to the Manitoba GenWeb query page.

Bartlett: http://www.mystic.mb.ca/mvickers/bartlett/index.html

Desautels: http://members.aol.com/marcjoli/Desautels.html

Dowd: http://www.mystic.mb.ca/mvickers/dowd/index.html

Fiola: http://members.aol.com/marcjoli/Fiola.html

Gagné: http://www.geocities.com/Heartland/Acres/3364/
The Story of Hilaire Gagné and Adéline Hibour [French only]
http://home.ican.net/~shsb/famillegagne.htm
The story of a branch of the family that immigrated to Manitoba in 1870. An insight into French immigration to Manitoba and early life in the new province.

Gervais: http://members.aol.com/marcjoli/Gervais.html

Jolicoeur: http://members.aol.com/marcjoli/Jolicoeur.html

McCormick: http://www.mccormickfamily.com/

Links to Your Canadian Past

Ontario and the Western Provinces

Ouimet: http://members.aol.com/marcjoli/Ouimet.html

Proteau: http://members.aol.com/marcjoli/Proteau.html

Rajotte: http://members.aol.com/marcjoli/Rajotte.html

Scurfield: http://www.familytreemaker.com/users/s/c/u/Robert-M-Scurfield/ODT2-0001.html

St. Jean: http://members.aol.com/marcjoli/StJean.html

Schmuland:
http://www.stat.ualberta.ca/people/schmu/family_history/family_history.html

Shiels: http://www.gatewest.net/~dshiels/

Syrenne/Cyrenne: [English & French]
http://www3.sympatico.ca/gpfern/EHOME.HTM

Vickers: http://www.mystic.mb.ca/mvickers/vickers/index.html

Chat Rooms and Mailing Lists

Manitoba Genealogy and History Mailing List:
majordomo@listserv.northwest.com
all: subscribe manitoba;
digest: subscribe manitoba-digest;
post: manitoba@listserv.northwest.com

Manitoba Query Forum Message Index
http://cgi.rootsweb.com/~genbbs/genbbs.cgi/Canada/Manitoba/General
View recent surname queries, post your own or subscribe to the mailing list.

Northwest Territories

Genealogical, Historical and Cultural Societies

Northwest Territories Genealogical Society
http://www.ssimicro.com/nonprofit/nwtgs/
Information on membership and meetings, plus a listing of active members with their research interests and e-mail addresses. The full text of the Newsletter *Inukshuk News* is also available.

Northwest Territories GenWeb Project
http://www.rootsweb.com/~cannt/nwt.htm
Under construction. Links to genealogical and territorial resources, indexed below.

Archives

Archive Centers

Archives of the Northwest Territories
http://pwnhc.learnnet.nt.ca/programs/archive.htm
Describes the holdings, collections, programs, exhibits and policies of the archives. Also provides a detailed schedule of territorial government records available for public consultation.

United Church Archives Network – Alberta and Northwest Conference Archives
http://www.uccan.org/archives/alberta.htm
Holds pre-1925 records for the Methodist, Presbyterian and Congregational churches and post-1925 records for the United Church of Canada for the Northwest Territories, including the congregations of Grace Church, Hay River, NT and Yellowknife Church, Yellowknife, NT.

<u>*Professional Organization*</u>

Northwest Territories Archives Council
http://pwnhc.learnnet.nt.ca/nwtac/nwtac.html
Dedicated to securing the establishment of archive repositories in the territory, fostering communications and training among members and increasing public and government awareness.

Libraries and Resource Centers

Library Web Sites for the Yukon and Northwest Territories
http://www.nlc-bnc.ca/canlib/eyunwt.htm
This site, provided by the National Library of Canada, lists links to the Web pages of public, university and government libraries in the territories.

Yellowknife Public Library
http://www.ssimicro.com/~xlibrary/
Includes a "Genealogy Reference Room," where the Northwest Territories Genealogical Society meets Wednesday nights. Contact information and hours listed.

Birth, Marriage, Death, Census and Other Data Online

Northwest Territories Vital Records
http://www.familytreemaker.com/00000159.html
The contact information for obtaining records from the territory, with scope of records.

Museums/Historic Sites & Groups

Museums and Historic Sites

Franklin Trail Homepage – province-wide
http://www.franklintrail.com/
Information on expeditions from 1993-1998 to search for evidence and artifacts of the last days of the Franklin expedition. Includes photos and a daily log from August 1998, as well as historical background on Franklin and his expeditions.

Prince of Wales Northern Heritage Center – Yellowknife, NWT
http://pwnhc.learnnet.nt.ca/
Dedicated to preserving the heritage and culture of the Inuit, Inuvialuit, Dene, Métis and non-aboriginal peoples of the Northwest. The Centre houses the territorial museum and archives and archaeological, educational and other programs.

Northern Life Museum and National Exhibition Centre – Fort Smith, NWT
http://susan.chin.gc.ca:8016/BASIS/guide/user/search/DDW?M=1&U=1&W=GUIDE_KEY=1281
Includes exhibits on the peoples of the North, northern wildlife and regional history.

Military, Native and Historic Groups

Tribes and Bands of Northwest Territories
http://hanksville.phast.umass.edu:8000/cultprop/contacts/tribal/NWT.html
A list of native groups in the territories, with contact information.

Territorial and Local History and Photos

Geographic Names Database
http://pwnhc.learnnet.nt.ca/programs/geodb.htm
This searchable database contains information on more than 11,000 names for geographic features in the Northwest Territories. Includes towns, lakes, rivers, mountains, etc.

Northern Vignettes
http://pwnhc.learnnet.nt.ca/ressec/nvindex.htm
These electronic "brochures," part of the Prince of Wales Northern Heritage Center, provide information on and photos of many historic sites in the territories, including Old Fort Reliance, Fort Hope, Fort Franklin, Old Fort Providence, Pelly Bay Church and Kellett's Storehouse.

Photograph Database
http://pwnhc.learnnet.nt.ca/programs/photodb.htm
A searchable database of over 20,000 images culled from the collection of the territorial archives. Low-resolution images with captions are provided, with prints and high-resolution files available for a fee.

City of Yellowknife: Facts
http://www.city.yellowknife.nt.ca/facts_frame.html
Includes the location, climate and history of the city, with photos.

Family Associations/Surnames

Northwest Territories GenWeb Surname Queries
http://cgi.rootsweb.com/~genbbs/genbbs.cgi/Canada/NWT/Genera l/
View recent or indexed queries or submit your own relating to NWT surnames.

Chat Rooms and Mailing Lists

Northern-Canada Mailing List [Yukon and NWT]: majordomo@listserv.northwest.com
all: subscribe northern-canada;
digest: subscribe northern-canada-digest

Ontario

Genealogical, Historical and Cultural Societies

Association for the Preservation of Ontario Land Registry Office Documents (APOLROD)
http://www.globalgenealogy.com/apolrod.htm
Formed to combat the planned dispersal or disposal of Registry documents from 1868-1955. Find out what you can do to help preserve these valuable heritage materials.

British Isles Family History Society of Greater Ottawa
http://www.cyberus.ca/~bifhsgo/
For researchers with origins in England, Ireland, Scotland, Wales, the Channel Islands and Isle of Man whose ancestors migrated to North America and settled in Canada.

Bruce County Genealogical Society
http://www.compunik.com/vmall/bcgs/index.htm
Includes a page on local resources available and Frequently Asked Questions.

Canadian Aviation Historical Society – Toronto Chapter [also see National society]
http://webhome.idirect.com/~cahstor/
Conducts 10 monthly meetings and publishes a monthly newsletter for aviation enthusiasts.

Cornwall Local Architectural Conservation Advisory Committee (LACAC)
http://www.cnwl.igs.net/~slm/corlacac.htm
Formerly Heritage Cornwall, this appointed committee advises the city council on heritage and preservation issues and maintains a list of registered properties in the city.

East Durham Historical Society – Hope Township and Northumberland County
http://www.nhb.com/edhs.htm
Information on membership, events, local tours, local history publications and more.

Esquesing Historical Society
HTTP://www.hhpl.on.ca/sigs/ehs/home.html
Includes a searchable index to their photo collection and links to old newspaper articles.

Halton Heritage Network
http://www.hhpl.on.ca/sigs/hhn/index.htm
An index of conservation/cultural/historical groups, libraries and museums in the Halton area.

Harrow Early Immigrant Research Society (HEIRS)
- http://www.rootsweb.com/~onheirs/index.htm
- http://www.cs.uwindsor.ca/gully/Heritage/HEIRSPG.HTM

Dedicated to studying and preserving the history and genealogy of the Township of Colchester South and the Town of Harrow in the county of Essex, Ontario.

Head of the Lakes Historical Society – Hamilton, ON
http://www.freenet.hamilton.on.ca/Information/associations/hlhs/
Society information and facts about Hamilton and the surrounding area.

Heritage Toronto
http://www.torontohistory.on.ca/
Formerly the Toronto Historical Board, this group operates 5 city museums, advises the city council on heritage and architectural issues and presents Toronto history to the public.

Icelandic Canadian Club of Toronto
http://web.idirect.com/~icct/
Includes membership info, events, meetings and an online newsletter.

Kent Historical Society
http://www.angelfire.com/az/kentontario/khs.html
Basic information on the society, its newsletter and upcoming events.

Kingston Irish Famine Commemoration Association
http://www.geocities.com/SoHo/Museum/7787/
Dedicated to researching the role of this town in the Irish potato famine.

Lanark County Genealogical Society
http://www.globalgenealogy.com/LCGS/
A comprehensive site on the society and genealogy and history of the county.

Leeds and Grenville Genealogical Society
http://www.cybertap.com/genealogy/
Info on meetings, membership, library holdings, reunions, speakers, publications, etc.

London and Middlesex Historical Society
http://www.fanshawec.on.ca/~Debra/intro1.htm
This site offers several full-length historical articles and stories on London and Middlesex County and also lists the Educational Programmes, Activities, Events and Projects that the society is involved in. Also included is "Jack Sharp's Archives – A Cave for Junior Historians."

London Transit Historical Socety
http://www.fanshawec.on.ca/~Debra/historical/ltc/lths.htm
Dedicated to preserving and promoting the contribution of the London Transit Commission and its predecessor companies to the city's history.

Millbrook and Cavan Historical Society
http://www.kawartha.net/~mchs/mchs.htm
Information on the society's objectives, publications and projects. Newsletter online.

Milton Historical Society
http://www.hhpl.on.ca/sigs/mhs/index.htm
Information on activities and events. Their archives collection is searchable online.

Ministry of Citizenship, Culture and Recreation: Historical Buildings and Sites in Ontario
http://www.gov.on.ca/MCZCR/english/culdiv/heritage/building.htm
Information on heritage and conservation statutes, programs and initiatives.

National Capital Genealogy Group
http://tor-pw1.netcom.ca/~trillium/ncgc/ncgcmain.html
A multi-cultural group promoting an interest in genealogy, family histories, heritage, and human migrations. The NCGG also offers courses in genealogy, history, computers, etc.

Norfolk Historical Society – Simcoe, ON
http://www.norfolklore.com/index.htm
Operates the Eva Brook Donly Museum, maintains a genealogical and historical library and publishes local histories and biographies.

Oakville Historical Society
http://www.oakvilleonline.com/670a.htm
Operates the Thomas House Museum and an archival collection of local history.

Ontario Genealogical Society
- **Main Page**: http://www.ogs.on.ca/
- **Branch Information**: http://www.ogs.on.ca/branches.htm

This site provides links to and information on the 29 branches of the provincial society and the activities, library information and publications of each branch. It also describes the ongoing cemetery, places of worship and census projects of the society.

Ontario GenWeb Project
http://www.multiboard.com/~spettit/ongenweb/
Information and links to genealogy for the entire province of Ontario, much of it indexed below. Links to over 50 county or district GenWeb pages, with lots of "how-to" and "where-to" info.

Ontario Heritage Foundation
http://www.heritagefdn.on.ca/home-eng.htm
An agency of the Ontario government, the OHF promotes and preserves the province's history in the form of built, cultural and natural heritage. The Foundation also administers the Historic Plaques program throughout Ontario.

Ontario Workers Arts and Heritage Center
http://www.web.net/~owahc/index.htm
Dedicated to preserving local working class history and organizing festivals, art displays and events that celebrate working life. The newsletter *Worklines* is available online.

St. Catherines Historical Society
http://www.niagara.com/~dmdorey/hssc/hssc.html
Information on the society, online newsletters, and local calendar of historical events.

Save Ontario Shipwrecks
http://yoda.sscl.uwo.ca:80/assoc/sos/
A province-wide association with local chapters, dedicated to preserving Ontario's marine heritage through shipwreck research and surveying, workshops and other programs.

Simcoe County Historical Association
http://www.bconnex.net/~scha/
Preserving the county's past with publications, events, meetings and historic plaques.

Slovenian Genealogical Society: Ontario Chapter
http://www.feefhs.org/slovenia/frgsgson.html
Contact information and links to the Slovenian Research List and "Slovenes in Canada."

Société Franco-Ontarienne d'Historie et Généalogie – Cornwall, ON [English & French]
http://www.glen-net.ca/sfohg/
Focuses on the Francophone presence in Ontario, with a large research collection and activities.

South Fredericksburgh Heritage Committee
http://www.l-a.on.ca/region/sfheritage.html
Preserving the cultural and built heritage of Lennox and Addington County with publications and projects, including restoring burial sites and photographing historic residences.

Stormont, Dundas and Glengarry Historical Society – Cornwall, ON
http://www.cnwl.igs.net/~slm/sd&ghs.htm
Operates the Inverardern Cottage Regency Museum, United Counties Museum (Wood House) and the society's own archives collection. Membership information available.

Temiskaming Genealogy Group
http://www.nt.net/~timetrav/
Includes the towns of Latchford, Cobalt, Haileybury, New Liskeard, Elk Lake, Matachewan, Gowganda, Earlton, Englehart, Tomstown, Kirkland Lake, Larder Lake and Virginiatown.

Toronto Cornish Association
http://www.digiserve.com/msyoung/tca.htm
Open to all Ontario researchers interested in ancestors from County Cornwall, UK.

Upper Ottawa Valley Genealogy Group
http://www.valleynet.on.ca/Culture/Genealogy/UOVGG/index.html
Serving Renfrew and Pontiac Counties. Newsletter, membership and library info online.

Waterloo Historical Society
http://dcs1.uwaterloo.ca/~marj/history/whs.html
Basic information on the society and its activities. Some information may be outdated.

Wellington County Historical Society
http://www.dcs.uwaterloo.ca/~marj/history/wellington.html
Basic information on the society and its publication, *Wellington History*.

Archives

Archive Centers

Archives of Ontario [English & French]
http://www.gov.on.ca/MCZCR/archives/
This site contains an entire section on doing genealogical research at the Archives of Ontario. It details the major genealogical holdings of the archives, how to use them and how to prepare for your visit or conduct research from a distance.

Lennox and Addington Museum and Archives: Archives Division
http://fox.nstn.ca/~museum/archives.html
Details the holdings of the Genealogical Research Library, Historical/Photograph/Newspaper Collections and Architectural and Environmental Research areas.

Ontario Jewish Archives – Toronto, ON
http://www.feduja.org/puzzled/infohigh/archives.stm
Preserving the history of Jewry in Ontario with manuscripts and printed documents, photos, films, audio recordings of oral histories and other heritage artifacts.

Peterborough City Archives
http://www.kawartha.net/~jleonard/archome.htm
An overview of the extensive holdings, finding aids, and description of genealogical resources. You can also search the archives' database online for genealogy, settlers, city records, etc.

Region of Peel Archives – Brampton, ON
http://www.region.peel.on.ca/heritage/archives.htm
Provides basic contact and research information, plus info on their research guide and holdings.

Renfrew Archives/Heritage Renfrew
http://www.renc.igs.net/~renarch/
Specializing in genealogy and history of the area around the town of Renfrew.

Simcoe County Archives Information
http://www.genweb.net/~simcoe/Archive.html
An overview of the holdings of the archives, with contact information.

United Church Archives Network: Montréal and Ontario Conference
http://www.uccan.org/archives/montreal.htm
Holds Methodist, Presbyterian and Congregational Church records for Carleton, Dundas, Glengarry, Prescott, Russell, and Stormont Counties prior to 1925, and United Church of Canada records for the same region after 1925.

United Church Archives Network: Manitoba and Northwest Ontario Conference Archives
http://www.uccan.org/archives/manitoba.htm
Holds Methodist, Presbyterian, and Congregational Church records from northwestern Ontario (esp. Cambrian Presbytery) prior to 1925, and United Church of Canada records after 1925.

Uxbridge-Scott Museum Archives
http://www.uxbridge.com/museum/research.html
A list of the resource materials available at the archives for vital, land, census and other records.

Waterloo - Conrad Grebel College/Mennonite Archives of Ontario: Genealogical Resources
http://www.lib.uwaterloo.ca/MHSC/gen.html
A categorized list of hodings, divided into: Databases, Books, Microfilms, Periodicals, Mennonite Cemetery Records, Bibles, Vital Event Registers, Family Genealogies.

Windsor Municipal Archives at the Windsor Public Library
http://www.city.windsor.on.ca/wpl/archives/
Municipal records for the City of Windsor and the communities of Ford City/East Windsor, Ojibway, Riverside, Sandwich, Walkerville and Sandwich East, West and South Twps.

Professional Organization

Archives Association of Ontario
http://www.fis.utoronto.ca/groups/aao/
Represents archival concerns in various levels of government, conducts educational programs, promotes professional standards and practices and facilitates communication between institutions and those who use archives for research.

Libraries and Research Centers

Directories and Catalogs

Library Websites and Catalogs: Ontario
http://www.nlc-bnc.ca/canlib/eontario.htm
Links to Internet, telnet and gopher sites for library information and catalogs in Ontario.

HYTELNET Library Catalogues: Ontario
http://moondog.usask.ca/hytelnet/ca0/ON.html
Links to telnet connections for libraries throughout the province, with instructions.

Family History Centres in Ontario
http://www.gov.on.ca/MCZCR/archives/english/geneal/fmlyhist.ht
m
A list of the addresses and contact information for the Family History Centres of the Church of Jesus Christ of Latter-Day Saints in Ontario.

Libraries and Research Centers

Belleville Public Library Genealogy Resources
http://www.rootsweb.com/~onhastin/genealog.htm
A listing of books, directories and other published information available at the library.

Elgin County Library Historical and Genealogical Collections
http://www.library.elgin-county.on.ca/~frank/history.html
Descriptions of and links to court records, clerk's and miscellaneous historical records available at the library, including scanned postcards of area towns.

Hamilton Public Library Special Collections
http://www.hpl.hamilton.on.ca/LOCAL/SPCOLL/Speccol.htm
Includes the Canadiana Collection, local history and archives collections.

Institut Franco-Ontarien: Laurentian University – Sudbury, ON
http://www.laurentian.ca/www/admn/grad_study/research/ifoe.html
Responsible for maintaining the J.N. Desmarais Library, hosting conferences and producing publications, including the journal *Revue du Nouvel-Ontario.*

Kingston – Stauffer Library, Queen's University: Genealogy Resources
http://stauffer.queensu.ca/inforef/guides/genealogy.htm
A list of the genealogy and history resources in the collection of the university's library and the Kingston Public library. Listed by category for the type and geographical origin of the resource.

Leamington Public Library Local History Projects
http://www.lccia.net/~lpl/english.htm
A description and search gateway to the LPL/Schoolnet local history projects.

London Public Library: London Room
http://discover.lpl.london.on.ca/service/londrm.htm
Houses the library's local history collection of materials on the counties of Middlesex, Elgin, Oxford and Norfolk (now part of Haldimand-Norfolk), with emphasis on the City of London.

Mississauga Library System Local History Collection
http://www.city.mississauga.on.ca/library/history/html/splocal.htm
An excellent, detailed introduction to the many resources in the Ruth Konrad Collection of Canadiana, containing materials on the development of the City of Mississauga, rural life in Ontario in the 1830's and ancestral history in Peel County.

Niagara Historical Resource Center – Niagara-on-the-Lake, ON
http://vaxxine.com/fa/notlpl/nhrc.htm
A permanent archive center of the Niagara-on-the-Lake Public Library, the center has an extensive collection of microfilmed historical material, plus numerous finding aids.

North York Public Library: Canadiana Collection
http://www.city.north-
york.on.ca/Library/Collections/Canadiana.html
Information on the holdings of this collection, which contains materials on the history of North York, Ontario and Canada, Genealogy-related works and archival materials.

Owen Sound Public Library Genealogy Resources
http://www.geocities.com/Heartland/4051/ospl.htm
A listing of the local history and genealogy materials available to researchers, with library hours.

Peterborough Public Library: Peterborough Collection
http://www.peterborough-library.com/peterborocoll.html
A collection of books, maps, photographs, microfilms, etc. relating to local history and heritage.

Toronto Reference Library: Genealogy and Local History
http://www.mtrl.toronto.on.ca/centres/spcoll/resource.htm
Detailing the library's collection of materials relating to biography, genealogy and history, "lists of persons" (cemetery, immigration, military lists, etc.) and research tools.

Wainfleet Township Public Library Genealogy Page
http://www.ont.net/wainfleet/library/genmain.htm
Includes a list of available resources, including cemetery and church records, demographic and census information, family histories and genealogies, local histories and research guides.

Birth, Marriage, Death, Census and Other Data Online

Directories/Multiple Databases

Genealogy Research in Ontario
http://www.xcelco.on.ca/~genealog/#Ontario
A brief overview of the various records available to researchers and where to find them.

Halton Local History Databases
http://www.hhpl.on.ca/localhistory/forms.htm
Search combined databases for local vital event, census, cemetery, land, employment, military and court records. Individual databases are indexed below in the appropriate sections.

Important Ontario Records for the Genealogist
http://www.ogs.on.ca/ontrecs.htm
This overview by the Ontario Genealogical Society details what records are available and in what time periods as well as where to find them. Covers vital, census, land and general records.

Ontario Genealogical Society Provincial Index
http://www.ogs.on.ca/ogspi/welcome.htm#welcome
This site provides access to an index, arranged by decade from 1850-1910, of a wide range of genealogical data dealing with families from Ontario. Data not only includes birth, marriage and death information, but also land, military, election, education and other records.

Ontario GenWeb Online Index of Ontario Resources
http://www.rootsweb.com/~canon/ogwoi/
A forum for posting and exchanging genealogical information relating to the province.

Vital Statistics and Parish Records

Birth, Marriage, Death Indexes for Ontario
http://www.geocities.com/Heartland/9332/bmd.htm
Provides the Archives of Ontario and LDS Family History Centers film numbers for records.

LDS Film Numbers for Ontario Birth Registrations
http://www.geocities.com/Heartland/9332/lds-b.htm
Film numbers for births, stillbirths and delayed registrations, with indexes, 1869-1899.

Office of the Registrar General: Birth and Other Certificates
[English and French]
http://www.ccr.gov.on.ca/mccr/orgindex.htm
Describes who can obtain a birth, marriage or death certificate from the Registrar General for an even that took place in Ontario and the process and fees for obtaining certificates.

Ontario Vital Records
http://www.familytreemaker.com/00000161.html
Addresses for where to write to obtain vital statistics records from Ontario.

Ontario Vital Statistics Bulletin
http://www.gov.on.ca/MCZCR/archives/english/geneal/vtlstats.ht
m
Information on how to research birth, marriage and death records at the Archives of Ontario.

***Bruce County Marriages* (1869-1873) Surname List**
http://members.aol.com/Winfieldpb/brucname.htm
A list of all surnames included in a published volume of marriages for this period.

District Marriage Registers
http://globalgenealogy.com/dismar2.htm
Hints for using these registers effectively in your research.

Erin Township (Wellington County) Records
http://www.chelmsford.com/home/priestner/Wellington.htm
Includes Births: 1874, 1882-83, 1896; Marriages: various records from 1831-1908 and Overland Marriages and Deaths from 1916 and 1921, as well as other various records.

Halton Area Births, Marriages and Deaths from Local Newspapers
http://www.hhpl.on.ca/localhistory/newssrch.htm
Search indexed vital records announcements from the *Acton Free Press, Burlington Gazette, Canadian Champion and Georgetown Herald.*

Lanark County Genealogical Society Transcribed Family Bibles
http://www.globalgenealogy.com/LCGS/LCGSDOCS.HTM#BIBLES

***Leamington Post* Newspaper Index**
http://www.lccia.net/~lpl/geneal.htm
Information extracted from birth, marriage and death announcements in the paper since 1907.

Montague Circuit (Montréal Conference) Methodist Church Membership Lists
http://www.globalgenealogy.com/LCGS/M-CHURCH.HTM
1903, 1904 and 1921 membership lists for Gillies', Pool's and Zion churches.

Nipissing District Vital Records
Extracted from early land records, many events relating to the Mattawa area.

- **Births (1871-1881)**: http://www.onlink.net/~twc/births.htm
- **Marriages (1871-1883)**: http://www.onlink.net/~twc/marriage.htm
- **Deaths (1871-1881)**: http://www.onlink.net/~twc/deaths.htm

Pakenham – St. Andrew's Presbyterian Church Communion Rolls (1896-1900)
http://www.globalgenealogy.com/LCGS/M-PAKSA.HTM

Perth Area Marriage Certificates
http://www.globalgenealogy.com/LCGS/LCGSDOCS.HTM#CERTS
Transcriptions of some records from the Perth museum for local families.

Ramsay Free Church Communion Rolls, 1846
http://www.globalgenealogy.com/LCGS/A-RAMSAY.HTM
A list of those who seceded from the Church of Scotland, the Auld Kirk, and founded the RFC.

St. Catharines Obituaries 1835-1938
http://www.niagara.com/~dmdorey/hssc/intro_obit.html
Excerpts from a book of local obituaries for St. Catharines and Niagara-on-the-Lake.

Death Cards From the Farmer and Salter Estates
http://www.globalgenealogy.com/LCGS/M-DEATH1.HTM
Surnames also include Brownlie, Burgess, Cavagnagh, Fergusson, MacNab and Willoughby.

Cemetery Information

Ontario Cemetery Finding Aid (OCFA)
http://www.antibe.com/ocfa/
A pointer database of 2 million interments throughout the entire province. Contains surname, cemetery name and location, with links/contact info for contributing organizations.

Bruce County Genealogical Society Cemetery Information
http://www.compunik.com/vmall/bcgs/bcgsceme.htm
A surname index to compiled cemetery transcriptions, with a list of local cemeteries transcribed.

Dundas and Lanark County Cemetery Lists
http://members.tripod.com/~GLENGARRY/CemList-Other.html
Locations of county cemeteries, with reference to published sources of transcriptions.

Glengarry County Cemetery Lists
Locations of county cemeteries, with reference to published sources of transcriptions.

- **North**: http://members.tripod.com/~GLENGARRY/CemList-Nglen.html
- **South**: http://members.tripod.com/~GLENGARRY/CemList-Sglen.html

Harrow and Colchester South Cemeteries
http://www.rootsweb.com/~onheirs/cemeteries.htm
Links to the indexes of several cemeteries in these two towns, with locations.

Hastings County Cemeteries
http://www.rootsweb.com/~onhastin/cemetery.htm
A list of cemeteries by township, many with an index to transcribed tombstones.

Index to the Cemeteries in Halton and Peel Counties
http://www.hhpl.on.ca/sigs/ogshp/cemtrans.htm
A searchable index of 14,107 surnames in 208 cemeteries in the two counties.

Lambton County Cemeteries
http://www.sarnia.com/groups/ogs/logs1.html
Links to download zipped index files of cemeteries in the communities of Bosanquet, Brooke, Dawn, Enniskillen, Euphemia, Moore, Plympton, Sarnia, Sombra and Warwick.

Lindsay – The Cemeteries of Lindsay, Ontario
http://www.sfn.saskatoon.sk.ca/iptest/james/index.html
Information and photos for St. Mary's Catholic and Riverside Cemeteries.

Lloydminster Cemetery Search
http://www.lloydminster.lib.sk.ca/cem1.htm
A searchable database created from information provided by the city clerk. Updated quarterly.

Middlesex County Cemetery Locations
http://www.mirror.org/groups/genealogy/cemetery.html
This list gives the township, cemetery name, concession and lot numbers.

Oxford County Cemetery List
http://www.geocities.com/Heartland/Acres/7990/Oxford_Cemeteries.html
A list of area cemeteries with concession and lot number, plus microfilm reel numbers.

Pakenham – Names of Those Believed to be Buried in Indian Hill Cemetery
http://www.globalgenealogy.com/LCGS/A-INDIAN.HTM
Names and burial date for interments where the gravesite is not known.

Peterborough County Cemetery List
http://home.kawartha.com/~d_millage/cemetary.htm
A list of the county's cemeteries and their locations, by township or community.

Prescott County Cemetery List
http://members.tripod.com/~GLENGARRY/CemListpc.html
Locations of county cemeteries, with reference to published sources of transcriptions.

Project Rose Garden
http://www.waynecook.com/rose.html
Transcriptions of gravestones in three pioneer cemeteries of Ontario: Two in Ponsonby – one for pioneer settlers from County Fermanagh, Ireland and one inscribed "Pioneer Cemetery 1843-1890." The third is Woodhill Pioneer Cemetery, or "Providence Primitive Methodist Cemetery."

Renfrew County Cemeteries
http://www.valleynet.on.ca/~aa127/uovgen/renfrew/Cemetery/countycem.html
A list of cemeteries by township, with alternate name, location and transcription information.

Stormont County Cemetery List
Locations of county cemeteries, with reference to published sources of transcriptions.

- **Cornwall & Finch**: http://members.tripod.com/~GLENGARRY/CemlistStor.html
- **Osnabruck & Roxborough**: http://members.tripod.com/~GLENGARRY/CemlistStorOR.html

Census Information/Settler and Voter Lists
Province-wide

1842 Census Headings
http://www.ogs.on.ca/mcgarry.htm
An explanation of the headings of each column from the original census, with examples.

1851 Ontario Census Indexes
http://www.rootsweb.com/~ote/1851in.htm
A list of published sources indexing the 1851 census. No online information.

1871 Census of Ontario – Index
http://www.archives.ca/db/1871/Introduction.html
A searchable index to the names of heads-of-household and individuals with a different surname living in the same house. Provides a reference to the page of the original microfilmed record, where other family members are listed.

1871 Census: Searchable Database of Heads and Strays
http://130.15.161.15/1871.htm
Contains a map of the census districts and explanations of codes used in the census.

Local Information

Barrie – 1837 "Census"
http://www.waynecook.com/1837.html
A list of people who were settled in Barrie (Simcoe County) in 1837.

Dalhousie Township and North Sherbrooke Voter Lists
- **1905**: http://www.globalgenealogy.com/LCGS/V-LK1905.HTM
- **1940**: http://www.globalgenealogy.com/LCGS/V-LK1940.HTM
- **Occupation Codes**: http://www.globalgenealogy.com/LCGS/V-OLIST.HTM
- **Post Office/Residence Codes**: http://www.globalgenealogy.com/LCGS/V-RLIST.HTM

Halton Area Censuses 1842-1901
http://www.hhpl.on.ca/localhistory/census.htm
Censuses for Acton, Esquesing and Georgetown from 1842, 51/52, 61, 71, 81, 91 and 1901.

Lanark Village Voter's List, 1875
http://www.globalgenealogy.com/LCGS/V-LK1875.HTM
- **Occupation Codes**: http://www.globalgenealogy.com/LCGS/V-OLIST.HTM
- **Post Office/Residence Codes**: http://www.globalgenealogy.com/LCGS/V-RLIST.HTM

Lanark County – Some British Pensioners Who Settled in Lanark County
http://www.globalgenealogy.com/LCGS/M-BPENS.HTM
The names of some of those who settled in the county between 1796 and 1837.

Malahide Township (Elgin County) 1842 Census Index
http://kanservu.ca/ptbruce/Genealogy/1842Census.html
A full transcription of the 1996 publication of the census, with 77 new entries.

Nipissing and Sudbury District 1891 Census Index
http://www.onlink.net/~twc/1891_census.htm
Provides a list of local surnames and information on how to conduct further research.

Oxford County Census Records
http://www.geocities.com/Heartland/Acres/7990/Oxford_Census.html
A list of census data available for each community, with microfilmed record numbers.

Perth County Census Record Microfilm Numbers
http://www.rootsweb.com/~onperth/filmnos.html
Microfilm reference numbers for the census records pertaining to towns in the county.

Perth Voter's Lists

- **1884**: http://www.globalgenealogy.com/LCGS/V-P1884.HTM
- **1898**: http://www.globalgenealogy.com/LCGS/V-P1898.HTM
- **1936**: http://www.globalgenealogy.com/LCGS/V-P1936.HTM
- **Occupation Codes**: http://www.globalgenealogy.com/LCGS/V-OLIST.HTM
- **Post Office/Residence Codes**: http://www.globalgenealogy.com/LCGS/V-RLIST.HTM

Perth Commercial Directory, 1936
http://www.globalgenealogy.com/LCGS/D-P1936.HTM
A transcription of the local business and residential directory.

Links to Your Canadian Past
Ontario and the Western Provinces

Peterborough – Searchable 1871 Census Index
http://www.archives.ca/db/1871/Peterborough/Peterborough_Search.html

Ross Township (Renfrew County) 1851 and 1871 Censuses
http://www.valleynet.on.ca/~aa127/uovgen/misc/rths.html#rthscen
Information and links for downloading information on heads of households and strays.

Passenger Lists/Immigration Data

1872 Ontario Immigration Information
http://www.dcs.uwaterloo.ca/%7Emarj/genealogy/emont1872.html
The text of an official Ontario Department of Agriculture and Public Works broadside, enticing British citizens to emigrate to Ontario. Contains information on passage, land and wages.

Migration of Voyageurs from Drummond Island to Penetanguishene in 1828
http://users.aol.com/bussineau/tree/drummond.html
A short article on the voyageurs who accompanied the British garrison, with a list of names.

Ontario Immigration (Into Ontario)
http://www.rootsweb.com/~canon/immigration.html
A list, by nationality, of the time period and locations of each group's immigration to Ontario.

Ottawa – A List of 19th Century German Immigrants in Ottawa
http://www.onlink.net/~twc/dfa.htm#A LIST OF 19TH CENTURY IMMIGRANTS IN OTTAWA
Provides the surname, given name, date and year of birth.

Paisley Townhead Emigration Society Lists

- http://www.globalgenealogy.com/LCGS/M-PAIS.HTM
- http://www.globalgenealogy.com/LCGS/A-PAIS.HTM

Lists of those recommended for emigration from Scotland and those who actually did emigrate aboard the *Earl of Buckingham* and settled in Ramsay Township.

Peter Robinson: Irish Emigration to Peterborough

- http://www.kawartha.net/~jleonard/robinson.htm

A historical overview and quicklist of surnames of Irish immigrants to the area.

- http://home.kawartha.com/~d_millage/probinsn.htm

A list of the dates the nine ships sailed from Cork, with passenger lists for each.

Prussian Immigrants Into the Ottawa Area

- http://www.dcs.uwaterloo.ca/~marj/genealogy/germanottawa.html
- http://dcs1.uwaterloo.ca/~marj/genealogy/germanottawa.html [same page]

Information from an 1861 Sessional Paper, including name, birthplace and where settled.

Migration/Emigration Data

Glengarry County –Connections: Glengarry County to . . . Various Locations on 3 Continents

http://members.tripod.com/~GLENGARRY/Connections.html

Indexed information on people from Glengarry who moved to other provinces, the U.S., etc.

Haldimand County – Migrations Out of Haldimand

http://www.rootsweb.com/~onhaldmi/mig.htm

A forum to post information on individuals and families who left the county.

Lanark County Genealogical Society: Community Histories of the Western Provinces
http://www.globalgenealogy.com/LCGS/A-CHIST.HTM
A compilation of data on people from Lanark County who emigrated to western Canadian provinces or states in the United States. Often gives information on birth/origin, etc.

Ontario Emigration (Out of Ontario)
http://www.globalgenealogy.com/LCGS/A-FR.HTM
A forum (under construction) for sharing information on those who left the province.

Land Records

Ontario Land Records
http://wwnet.com/~treesrch/ontland.html
An excellent article on what types of records are available and how to find and use them.

Ontario Land Registry Offices
http://www.globalgenealogy.com/apolrod6.htm
A list of all the Land Registry Offices located throughout the province.

Upper Canada Land Records Index
http://www.archives.ca/www/svcs/english/INDEXRG1_E.html#U pper Canada
A finding aid for both the Land Books and Land Petitions for the provinces of Upper Canada, 1791-1841, and Canada, 1841-1867.

Erin Township Land Records 1877
http://www.chelmsford.com/home/priestner/Land.htm
A list of farms and their owners from the 1877 Atlas of Waterloo Wellington Counties.

Georgetown Land Records Index
http://www.hhpl.on.ca/localhistory/landsrch.htm
A searchable index of the first 2 volumes of "Abstract Index to Deeds" for Georgetown, Ontario.

Haldimand County Land Records Film Numbers
http://www.rootsweb.com/~onhaldmi/land.htm
A table of land records pertaining to the county, with corresponding microfilm numbers.

Lavant Township Land Records Index
http://www.globalgenealogy.com/LCGS/M-LAVIX.HTM
Covers the period from the 1830's to the early 1900's.

Nipissing District Crown Land Grants
http://www.onlink.net/~twc/grants.htm
Includes the lot, concession, township and microfiche location for early 20th century grants.

North Sherbrook Township Land Records Index
http://www.globalgenealogy.com/LCGS/M-NSRIX.HTM
Covers the period from the 1830's to the early 1900's.

Ramsay Township Cess Rolls, 1837
http://www.globalgenealogy.com/LCGS/M-RCESS.HTM

Wainfleet Township (Welland County) Land Concessions 1795
http://www.rootsweb.com/~pictou/wnflt.htm
A list of concessions from section 2 of 2 of M. Burwall's Map No. 21 T.D, undated.

Employment/Professional Information

Blacksmith's Price List 1912
http://www.globalgenealogy.com/LCGS/M-BLACK.HTM
Prices for services of Perth area blacksmiths, with the names of the local blacksmiths.

Constables, 1861
http://www.globalgenealogy.com/LCGS/M-CONST.HTM
A list of those appointed in the General Quarter Sessions at Perth in March, with towns served.

Halton's Historical Directories
http://www.hhpl.on.ca/localhistory/histdir.asp
Searchable index to several directories of local businessmen and farmers, 1851-1898.

Lanark County Commercial Directory 1881/2
http://www.globalgenealogy.com/LCGS/D-LK1880.HTM
Includes the name of the person and their business, mostly in the town of Perth.

Lanark County Teachers, 1898
http://www.globalgenealogy.com/LCGS/A-TEACH.HTM
Extracted from the Perth *Courier*, February 4, 1898.

Legal and Other Data

Elgin County Clerk Records
http://www.library.elgin-county.on.ca/~frank/COUNTY.TXT
Descriptions of the contents of a collection of various county clerk records.

Elgin County Surrogate Court Records
http://www.library.elgin-county.on.ca/~frank/estate.html
Index of London District (up to 1853) and Elgin County records from 1800-1900.

Erin Township (Wellington County) Surrogate Court Records
http://www.chelmsford.com/home/priestner/Wellington.htm
Links to transcriptions from eight court books covering the period 1840-1880.

Halton Area Local Histories
http://www.hhpl.on.ca/localhistory/LHBooks.asp
A searchable index to several local history books for Acton, Esquesing and Georgetown.

Halton County Surrogate Court Records Index
http://www.hhpl.on.ca/localhistory/Surrsrch.htm
Searchable index to probate court documents, including wills, from 1855-1900.

Hastings County Wills and Estate Records
http://www.tbaytel.net/bmartin/wills-14.htm
A table of Estate Records, dates and corresponding microfilm reel numbers for county records.

Lanark County Wills
http://www.globalgenealogy.com/LCGS/A-WILLS.HTM
Surnames extracted from wills from 1868, 1895 and 1935 for Lanark Township, Town of Almonte and the General Register.

Marine Heritage Database
http://yoda.sscl.uwo.ca:80/assoc/sos/dbase.html
A browseable database of shipwrecks, maps, photos, marine artifacts, publications, institutions and a glossary of marine heritage terms.

Nipissing District Wills on Microfilm
http://www.onlink.net/~twc/wills.htm
A finding aid giving the Estate File number, dates covered and microfilm reference numbers.

Museums/Historic Sites/Groups

Directories/Guides

Directory of Ontario Museums
http://www.museumassn.on.ca/dir.htm
Search the directory alphabetically or by city, museum type or provincial travel region.

Brant County Museums and Galleries
http://www.bfree.on.ca/comdir/musgal/musgal.htm
A list of local institutions, with brief descriptions and contact information.

Lanark County Museums
http://www.globalgenealogy.com/LCGS/LCGSMUSE.HTM
A brief overview of several museums located throughout the county, with contact information.

Museums and Historic Sites

Ameliasburgh Historical Museum
http://www.pec.on.ca/ameliasburghmuseum/
A heritage village with blacksmith, sap shanty, log cabin, farm machinery and other buildings.

Battlefield House Museum – Stoney Creek, ON
http://alpha.binatech.on.ca/~bhmchin/
Costumed interpreters present the early 19th century life of the Gage family in this homestead set in a 32-acre park that was the site of the Battle of Stoney Creek.

Battle of the Windmill National Historic Site – Prescott, ON
[English & French]
http://parkscanada.pch.gc.ca/parks/ontario/battle_windmill/battle_windmille.htm

Links to Your Canadian Past
Ontario and the Western Provinces

Bellevue House National Historic Site – Kingston, ON [English & French]
http://parkscanada.pch.gc.ca/parks/ontario/bellevue_house/bellevue_housee.htm
The restored 1840's home of Prime Minister John A. MacDonald, with costumed interpreters.

Benares House and Visitors Center – Mississauga, ON
http://www.city.mississauga.on.ca/commsvcs/heritage/html/ben.htm
The early 20th century Georgian-style home of four generations of the Harris and Sayers families.

Bethune Memorial House – Gravenhurst, ON [English & French]
http://parkscanada.pch.gc.ca/parks/ontario/bethune_memorial_house/bethune_memorial_housee.htm
A restored 1890's Victorian manse, birthplace of renowned military doctor Norman Bethune.

Billings Estate Museum – Ottawa, ON
http://susan.chin.gc.ca:8016/BASIS/guide/user/search/DDW?M=1&U=1&W=GUIDE_KEY=650
The home of 5 generations of the Billings family is the oldest residence in Ottawa. Inside, 200 years of family and community history are told through displays of over 24,000 artifacts.

Billy Bishop Museum – Owen Sound, ON
http://www.greycounty.on.ca/museum/bishmus.html
Dedicated to the memory of a local WWI flying ace, the museum presents artifacts from World War I and World War II and a video viewing room featuring peace and wartime aviation themes.

Links to Your Canadian Past

Ontario and the Western Provinces

Black Creek Pioneer Village – North York, ON
http://www.city.north-york.on.ca/Culture/Pioneer.html
A recreated 1860's village with costumed interpreters performing daily tasks and trades.

Bois Blanc Island Lighthouse National Historic Site – Amherstburg, ON [English & French]
http://parkscanada.pch.gc.ca/parks/ontario/bois_blanc_lths/bois_blanc_lthse.htm

Bowmanville Museum – Clarington, ON
http://susan.chin.gc.ca:8016/BASIS/guide/user/search/DDW?M=1&U=1&W=GUIDE_KEY=1609
A late Victorian house with exhibits depicting the life of a merchant family from 1901 to 1930.

Bradley Museum – Mississauga, ON
http://www.city.mississauga.on.ca/commsvcs/heritage/html/brad.htm
The restored 19th century home of a United Empire Loyalist depicts everyday life of early settlers. Costumed interpreters enact the seasonal chores of a family living off the land.

Brant County Museum and Archives – Brantford, ON
http://bfree.on.ca/comdir/musgal/bcma/index.htm

Brockville Museum – Brockville, ON
http://www.cybertap.com/bmchin/index.htm
Local history exhibits include Brockville and the River City, Brockville and the Homefront, Brockville: "Detroit East" and Made in Brockville.

Bruce County Museum – Southampton, ON
http://www.brucecounty.on.ca/indexm.htm
Six galleries depicting the county in prehistoric times, aboriginal history, the first European settlers and military, marine and agricultural influences on Bruce County's society.

Butler's Barracks National Historic Site – Niagara-on-the-Lake, ON [English & French]
http://parkscanada.pch.gc.ca/parks/ontario/butlers_barracks/butlers_barrackse.htm
This site depicts 150 years of military history in Ontario.

Buxton Historic Site and Museum – North Buxton, ON
http://www.ciaccess.com/~jdnewby/museum.htm
A Black historical settlement that was the site of the original Elgin settlement, and the last stop for many African Americans on their journey on the Underground Railroad.

Campbell House – Toronto, ON
http://www.advsoc.on.ca/campbell/index.html
A brief history and virtual tour of the 1822 home of local dignitary Sir William Campbell.

Clarke Museum and Archives – Clarington, ON
http://susan.chin.gc.ca:8016/BASIS/guide/user/search/DDW?M=1&U=1&W=GUIDE_KEY=1608
Exhibits and archives on the local history of Clarke and Darlington, both now part of Clarington.

Cobalt Mining Museum – Cobalt, ON
http://server1.nt.net/cobalt/minemus.htm
Mining and prospecting equipment and artifacts help tell the story of this former mining town.

Links to Your Canadian Past

Ontario and the Western Provinces

Coldwater Canadiana Museum – Coldwater, ON
http://www.waynecook.com/coldwater.html
A brief description of the Woodrow Homestead, a pioneer log home that belonged to Archibald Woodrow and his family, from Scotland.

County of Grey/Owen Sound Museum – Owen Sound, ON
http://www.greycounty.on.ca/museum/
Presents the rural history of the county from 1815 to 1930. Features seven heritage buildings, including a blacksmith shop, automotive garage, barn and an Ontario-style farmhouse.

Cumberland Heritage Village Museum – Cumberland, ON
http://www.municipality.cumberland.on.ca/en/museum.html
A recreated village with costumed interpreters, focusing on industrialization and transportation.

Doon Heritage Crossroads – Kitchener, ON
http://www.region.waterloo.on.ca/doon/
A living history museum with a recreated rural village, two farms and costumed interpreters.

Dorothy's House Museum – Garden Hill, ON
http://www.nhb.com/museum.htm
A restored Victorian-style home built by a local carpenter. Also includes a barn and drive shed featuring carpentry and woodworking tools, as well as furniture made by local craftsmen.

Dundurn Castle – Hamilton, ON
http://www.city.hamilton.on.ca/cultureandrecreation/dundern.html
Costumed interpreters lead you through 40 rooms on three floors of the former home of Sir Allan McNab, one of Canada's early Premiers.

Dryden and District Museum – Dryden, ON
http://server.awcoldstream.com/drydenmuseum/

Dufferin County Museum and Archives – Orangeville, ON
http://www.flexnet.com/~unique/dcn/dcm.htm
Tour a replica log house, Orange Lodge and CPR flag station at this community museum, which includes a four-floor museum building and local heritage archives.

Edinburgh Square Heritage and Cultural Centre – Caledonia, ON
http://www.headstartcomp.on.ca/heritage/square/
Exhibits depicting the history of the town of Caledonia from its native and Loyalist settlement.

Elgin County Museums – St. Thomas, ON
http://www.execulink.com/~ecpmchin/

- **Pioneer Museum**:
  http://www.execulink.com/~ecpmchin/about.htm
- **Military Museum**:
  http://www.execulink.com/~ecpmchin/emm.htm

Eva Brook Donly Museum – Simcoe, ON
http://www.norfolklore.com/
Set in an 1840's Georgian style home, the museum presents paintings, antiques and exhibits depicting the history of Norfolk County, Ontario.

Fort George National Historic Park – Niagara-on-the-Lake, ON

- http://www.niagara.com/~parkscan/
- http://parkscanada.pch.gc.ca/parks/ontario/fort_george/fort_georgee.htm

A British fort that was the main headquarters of the British Army in Ontario, a depot for the Provincial Marine and the scene of battles during the War of 1812.

Fort Henry – Kingston, ON
http://www.forthenry.kingston.net/
A restored former British Army fort located at the entrance to the Rideau Canal.

Fort Malden National Historic Site – Amherstburg, ON
[English & French]
http://parkscanada.pch.gc.ca/parks/ontario/fort_malden/fort_maldene.htm
An original 1819 barracks and 1840's earthworks at this site, along with a modern visitors' center, depict the forts roles as army garrison, British Indian Department post and dockyard.

Fort Mississauga National Historic Site – Niagara-on-the-Lake, ON [English & French]
http://parkscanada.pch.gc.ca/parks/ontario/fort_mississauga/fort_mississaugae.htm

Fort St. Joseph National Historic Site – Richards Landing, ON
[English & French]
http://parkscanada.pch.gc.ca/parks/ontario/fort_st-joseph/fort_st-josephe.htm
The stabilized remains of the westernmost outpost in British North America. The fort was headquarters of the Indian Department, a fur trade depot and active in the War of 1812.

Fort Wellington National Historic Site – Prescott, ON [English & French]
http://parkscanada.pch.gc.ca/parks/ontario/fort_wellington/fort_wellingtone.htm
Restored ramparts and buildings that served during the War of 1812 and 1837-38 Rebellions.

Glanmore National Historic Site / Hastings County Museum – Belleville, ON
http://www.quinte.net/glanmore/
Local history displays include an 1870's general store, pre-Confederation homestead and upper class furnishings and art.

Glengarry Cairn National Historic Site– Prescott, ON [English & French]
http://parkscanada.pch.gc.ca/parks/ontario/glengarry_cairn/glengarry_cairne.htm
Erected by the Glengarry Militia to commemorate the suppression of the 1837-38 Rebellions.

The Grimsby Museum – Grimsby, ON
http://www.town.grimsby.on.ca/museum.html
Depicting local history, including prehistory and the founding of "The Forty" by Loyalists.

Guelph Civic Museum – Guelph, ON
http://www.museum.guelph.on.ca/guelph.htm
Over 30,000 artifacts, 4,000 photos and archival materials tracing the economic, social and cultural history of the city since its founding in 1827.

Haliburton Highlands Museum – Haliburton, ON
http://www.auriga.on.ca/hal/museum.html
Local native history, early settlement, lumbering, railway, farmstead and homestead exhibits.

Halton County Radial Railway – Milton, ON
http://www.hcry.org/
"Ontario's operating streetcar museum." Ride through 2km of scenic woodlands.

Halton Region Museum – Milton, ON
http://museum.region.halton.on.ca/
Located in the Kelso Conservation Area, the HRM displays local natural and cultural history.

Hamilton – A Brief History of the Custom House
http://www.web.net/~owahc/1332.htm
An overview of the history of this building and its changing roles from 1855 through 1979.

Hamilton Museum of Steam and Technology
http://www.city.hamilton.on.ca/cultureandrecreation/steam.html
Housing two 70-ton steam engines, the museum also presents regional industrial history.

Heritage House Museum – Smiths Falls, ON
http://www.town.smiths-falls.on.ca/heritage.htm
The restored 1862 home of local pioneer and mill owner Joshua Bates.

Heritage Silver Trail – Colbalt, ON
http://www.nt.net/cobalt/trail.htm
A self-guiding tour through the silver mining camp at Cobalt and the surrounding area.

Historic Plaques of Ontario – Province-wide
http://www.waynecook.com/historic.html
The location and full text of 110 historic plaque markers located throughout the province. Links to sites of related interest to the subjects of the plaques.

HMCS HAIDA Naval Museum – Toronto, ON
http://www3.sympatico.ca/hrc/haida/home.htm
Tour the last surviving Tribal class destroyer and view exhibits on Canadian naval history.

HMS Detroit Project, Inc./Gordon House – Amherstburg, ON
http://www.x5ca.net/~hmsdet/
Dedicated to the maritime heritage of Amherstburg and building a replica of the *Detroit.*

Huron County Museum and Historic Gaol – Goderich, ON
http://www.huroned.edu.on.ca/Museum/frames.htm
Depicting local commercial development, agriculture, decorative arts and the military.

Inverarden House National Historic Site– Prescott, ON
[English & French]
http://parkscanada.pch.gc.ca/parks/ontario/inverarden_house/inverarden_housee.htm

Jordan Historical Museum of the Twenty – Jordan, ON
http://www.tourismniagara.com/jordanmuseum/
A log home and former schoolhouse depicting the role of Mennonites in Jordan history.

Joseph Schneider Haus Museum and Gallery – Kitchener, ON
http://www.region.waterloo.on.ca/jsh/index.html
The farmhouse of a Pennsylvania-German Mennonite settler. Includes the Canadian Harvest Collection of German-Canadian Folk Art and artifacts from Canadian Germanic settlement.

Kingston City Hall
http://www.kingston.net/iknet/alliance/cityhall.html
Excerpts from several publications detailing the history of this stately structure.

Kingston Martello Towers National Historic Site – Kingston, ON [English & French]

- http://parkscanada.pch.gc.ca/parks/ontario/kingston_m_tower/kingston_m_towere.htm
- http://www.kingston.net/iknet/alliance/murney.html

British masonry fortifications dating from the mid 19th century.

Komoka Railway Museum – Komoka, ON
http://www.komokarail.ca/
The railway history of southwestern Ontario, including the Canadian National, Canadian Pacific and Grand Trunk Railways. Includes a 1913 steam logging locomotive.

Lake of the Woods Museum – Kenora, ON
http://netra.voyageur.ca/~lwmchin/museum.html
Dedicated to the history of Kenora (formerly Rat Portage), Keewatin and Lake of the Woods, in the areas of exploration, settlement, population, education, arts, trade, transportation, etc.

Lambton Heritage Museum – Grand Bend, ON
http://www.grandbend.com/lambton/museum.htm
Photos and information on this museum, which presents the county's human and natural history.

Lang Pioneer Village – Peterborough, ON
http://www.ftsw.com/pioneer/
20 heritage buildings set in a 25-acre lot with gardens, farmyard animals and costumed interpreters as a tinsmith, carpenter, printer, blacksmith and other pioneer trades.

Laurier House National Historic Site – Ottawa, ON [English & French]
http://parkscanada.pch.gc.ca/parks/ontario/laurier_house/laurier_housee.htm
The 1878 Victorian house that was the residence of two successive prime ministers: Sir Wilfrid Laurier and William Lyon Mackenzie King.

Lennox and Addington County Museum and Archives – Napanee, ON
http://fox.nstn.ca/~museum/
Features over 10,000 local artifacts of furniture, textiles, clothing, toys, transportation, tools, etc.

London Museum of Archaeology – London, ON
http://www.uwo.ca/museum/
Devoted to the study, display, and interpretation of the human occupation of Southwestern Ontario over the past 11,000 years.

Lundy's Lane Historical Museum – Niagara Falls, ON
http://www.fallscasino.com/museum/

Macaulay Heritage Park – Picton, ON
http://www.pec.on.ca/macaulay/
Includes the 1830 Macaulay home, the old Church of St. Mary Magdalene (now the Prince Edward County Museum), St. Mary Magdalene Cemetery and Heritage Gardens.

MacLachlan Woodworking Museum – Kingston, ON
http://ma1.rmc.ca/museum/
Exhibits focusing on tree harvesting and woodworking tools and trades in pioneer Ontario.

Macpherson House – Napanee, ON
http://novatech.on.ca/napanee/mcpher.html
The Georgian style home of Napanee founder Allan Macpherson, cousin of John A. MacDonald.

Mariners Park Museum – Milford, ON
http://www.stormy.ca/perc/marmus.html
Artifacts and archival material relating to the nautical history of Ontario and the Great Lakes.

Maritime Museum of the Great Lakes – Kingston, ON
- http://www.marmus.ca/marmus/
- http://www.marmus.ca/marmus/pumphouse.html

Exhibit galleries, a workshop, library and archives housed in a renovated historic shipyard. The museum also includes the Pump House Steam Museum and the icebreaker Alexander Henry.

Markham Museum – Markham, ON
http://www.city.markham.on.ca/rec/museum.htm
Twenty-five acres of historic buildings and modern exhibits, including horse-drawn vehicles.

Marsh Collection Society – Amherstburg, ON
http://www.rootsweb.com/~onessex/marsh.htm
This museum/archives contains photographs, artifacts and archival and genealogical material relating to the Town of Amherstburg, Lower Detroit River district and the Great Lakes.

Mattawa and District Museum – Mattawa, ON
http://www.city.north-bay.on.ca/mattawa/mw-m&dm.htm
Exhibits on local aboriginal peoples, early settlement, and a walking tour of the town.

McCrae House – Guelph, ON
http://www.museum.guelph.on.ca/mccrae.htm
Dedicated to the life and family of John McCrae, physician and professor of medecine, who was the author of the WWII poem "In Flanders Fields," while in the Canadian Army Medical Corps.

Meaford Museum – Meaford, ON
http://www.greycounty.on.ca/museum/mmus.htm
Presents the history of Meaford, its maritime heritage and ties to the Great Lakes.

Metropolitan Toronto Police Museum – Toronto, ON
http://www.mtps.on.ca/cos/cpsmusem.html
Self-guiding, interactive exhibits lead the visitor through police history from the 1800's to today.

Mill of Kintail Museum and Conservation Area – Almonte, ON
http://www.perth.igs.net/~library/kintail/
The sculptures, memorabilia and collection of pioneer artifacts of Robert T. McKenzie.

Montgomery's Inn- Toronto, ON
http://www.bigham.ca/montgomery/
A comprehensive site about the 1840's inn run by Thomas Montgomery and his family. Find information on the Montgomery family, inn, events and tours – or take an online tour of the inn.

Musée Sturgeon River House Museum – Nipissing, ON
http://www.city.north-bay.on.ca/west_nip/msrhm.htm
This former fur trading post now depicts the history of the fur trade in the area.

Muskoka Lakes Museum – Port Carling, ON
http://www.muskoka.com/tourism/mlm/
Collections of marine history, glassware, pioneer tools and equipment, photographs, etc.

Myrtleville House Museum – Brantford, ON
http://www.bfree.on.ca/comdir/musgal/myrtle/
The restored 1838 home of an immigrant Irish family, with household and farming artifacts.

Navy Island National Historic Site – Niagara-on-the-Lake, ON
[English & French]
http://parkscanada.pch.gc.ca/parks/ontario/navy_island/navy_islande.htm
Located on the site of the first British shipyard to serve the upper Great Lakes.

Nepean Museum – Nepean, ON
http://www.nepeanmuseum.on.ca/
Take a "Virtual Walking Tour" through this museum displaying local history artifacts.

Nepean – Log Farm and Log Tavern Artifacts
http://citd.scar.utoronto.ca/CITD/Instructional/Archaelogy/Canadian-Archaeology/CanArch.html
Photos and text depicting the discovery of 19th-century log structures in Nepean, with history.

Nipissing Township Museum – Nipissing, ON
http://www.city.north-bay.on.ca/almaguin/nipising.htm
Recreated pioneer homes and shops and an original log church recount the town's history.

North Bay Area Museum – North Bay, ON
http://www.city.north-bay.on.ca/museum/main.htm
Includes information on and photographs of local history exhibits.

North Bay Historic Sites and Monuments – North Bay, ON
http://www.city.north-bay.on.ca/history/monument.htm
A list of historic locations and commemorative markers throughout the town.

North Himsworth Museum – Callender, ON
http://www.city.north-bay.on.ca/almaguin/himswrth.htm
Visit the Olde Tyme Barber Shop, view logging exhibits and photos and Dionne Quints exhibits.

Oakville Museum – Oakville, ON
http://susan.chin.gc.ca:8016/BASIS/guide/user/search/DDW?M=1&U=1&W=GUIDE_KEY=928
Recounts the history of Oakville through the Chisholms, a founding family. The Erchless Estate, Custom House and Coach House display over 130 years of artifacts and family belongings.

Ontario Tobacco Museum and Heritage Center – Delhi, ON
http://www.tcin.net/dotm/index.html
This museum not only houses collections relating to the tobacco industry, but also local history for the town of Delhi and the surrounding region, including a streetscape of historic buildings.

Oshawa Community Museum and Archives – Oshawa, ON
http://www.worldsites.net/oshawamuseum/
Local history exhibits and artifacts housed in three mid-1800's buildings on Oshawa's lakefront.

Ottawa – St. Patrick's Basilica: A Guided Tour
http://infoweb.magi.com/~seanj/basilica/index.html
Take an online tour (inside and out) of the oldest English-speaking Catholic church in Ottawa.

Owen Sound Marine-Rail Museum – Owen Sound, ON
http://www.geocities.com/Athens/Delphi/6265/
Features artifacts, models and photos of local marine and rail transportation, but also the woodworking, cement and shipbuilding industries supported by these sectors.

Peel Heritage Complex – Brampton, ON
http://www.region.peel.on.ca/heritage/hcomplex.htm
Includes the Region of Peel Museum, with local history exhibits, programs and events.

Penetanguishene Centennial Museum – Penetanguishene, ON
http://www.huronet.com/penetang/2584new_site/museum/
The past of "the most historic town west of Québec City" is displayed in a former lumber office.

Perth Museum – Perth, ON
http://www.perth.igs.net/~perth/musmain.htm
Period rooms and exhibits in an 1840's merchants home depicting Perth's past.

Peterborough Museum – Peterborough, ON
http://www.kawartha.net/~jleonard/musehome.htm
Over 22,000 artifacts relating to the city of Peterborough are on display, including textiles and quilts, furniture, military artifacts, metal toys, clocks, appliances and locally-built canoes.

Petrolia Discovery – Petrolia, ON
http://town.petrolia.on.ca/discovery/index.html
View active displays of Ontario's oil history. This living heritage site contains working oil wells from over 100 years ago, with a central power plant and jerker rods going out to each rig.

Pickering Museum Village – Greenwood, ON
http://www.town.pickering.on.ca/Museum/content.html
Fourteen heritage buildings depicting everyday life in Pickering township in the 1830's.

The Pier – Toronto, ON
http://www.torontohistory.on.ca/thepier/thepier.html
Interactive displays, exhibits and rare artifacts depicting the history of Toronto Bay.

Pinhey's Point – Kanata, ON
http://infoweb.magi.com/~hammelsh/pinhey.html
An 88-acre heritage site, centered around the 1820's Ottawa River home of Hamnett Pinhey.

Point Clark Lighthouse National Historic Site – Kitchener, ON
[English & French]
http://parkscanada.pch.gc.ca/parks/ontario/point_clark_lths/point_clark_lthse.htm
An 1850's "Imperial" limestone tower overlooking Lake Huron.

Port Colborne Historical and Marine Museum – Port Colborne, ON
http://susan.chin.gc.ca:8016/BASIS/guide/user/search/DDW?M=1&U=1&W=GUIDE_KEY=1120
A maritime museum and heritage village located on the Welland Canal. Historic buildings include a blacksmith, log home and schoolhouse, Tea Room and Tug Boat Wheelhouse.

Queenston Heights National Historic Site – Niagara-on-the-Lake, ON [English & French]
http://parkscanada.pch.gc.ca/parks/ontario/queenston_heights/queenston_heightse.htm

Railway and Pioneer Museum – Cochrane, ON
http://www.northernc.on.ca/net-11/edcoch/pion.htm
Railway memorabilia housed in actual train cars, honoring the pioneers of northern Ontario.

Red Lake Museum – Red Lake, ON
http://susan.chin.gc.ca:8016/BASIS/guide/user/search/DDW?M=1&U=1&W=GUIDE_KEY=1472
Exhibits recounting the history of the fur trade, gold mining, bush pilots and First Nations.

Rideau Canal National Historic Site – Kingston to Ottawa [English & French]
http://parkscanada.pch.gc.ca/parks/ontario/rideau_canal/rideau_canale.htm
Stretching 202 kilometers from Kingston to Ottawa, the Rideau is a series of lakes, rivers and canals – still navigable – that played an important role in early transportation.

Rideau Hall – Ottawa, ON
http://www.gg.ca/visitor_e.html
The official residence of Canada's Governor General since 1867.

Ron Morel Memorial Museum – Kapuskasing, ON [French only]
http://www.intergov.gc.ca/mun/on/kap/attractf.html
Houses steam train #1507 and its cars, as well as exhibits on the fur trade and the railway.

Royal Ontario Museum – Toronto, ON [English & French]
http://www.rom.on.ca/
Art, Archaeology and Science exhibits. Includes a floor of Canadian Heritage exhibits.

Saint-Louis Mission National Historic Site – Honey Harbour, ON [English & French]
http://parkscanada.pch.gc.ca/parks/ontario/st-louis_mission/st-louis_missione.htm
The site of a former Huron village and Jesuit mission that was attacked by the Iroquois in 1649.

St. Marys Museum – St. Marys, ON
http://www.stonetown.net/museum/index.html
Exhibits and archival materials relating to the history of the town and people of St. Marys.

Sault Ste. Marie Canal National Historic Site – Sault Ste. Marie, ON [English & French]
http://parkscanada.pch.gc.ca/parks/ontario/sault_st-marie_canal/sault_st-marie_canale.htm
An online tour, history and photos of this historic 1890's canal, powerhouse and swing dam.

Sault Ste. Marie Heritage Buildings – Sault Ste. Marie, ON
http://www.sault-canada.com/houses.html
Short text and photos of historical buildings and locations throughout the town.

Scarborough Historical Museum – Scarborough, ON
http://www.city.scarborough.on.ca/mm/dir/depts/deptrpc/facility/museum/museum.html
Set in the Thomson Memorial Park, the museum includes the 1850's Cornell House, McCowan Log House, Hough Carriage Works and Kennedy Annex, depicting life in the late 1800's.

School House Museum – Meilleur's Bay, Point Alexander, ON
http://www.intranet.ca/~dlemire/Schoolhouse/
Tells the history of Deep River and the surrounding area with artifacts and photographs.

Scugog Shores Historical Museum – Port Perry, ON
http://www.durham.net/~ssh-chin/
Ten restored 19th-century buildings and displays depicting local lifestyles, commerce and industry. On special event days, costumed interpreters re-enact trades and crafts.

Sesquicentennial Museum and Archives – Toronto, ON
http://susan.chin.gc.ca:8016/BASIS/guide/user/search/DDW?M=1&U=1&W=GUIDE_KEY=1521
Presents the history of public education in Toronto in exhibits and archival material.

Sharon Temple Historic Site and Museum – Sharon, ON
http://home.interhop.net/~aschrauwe/sharon.html
The magnificent Temple of the Children of Peace, along with the 1819 Doan house and outbuildings and 1829 "Study." The library includes genealogical info on the founders.

Sir Harry Oakes Chateau Museum of Northern History – Kirkland Lake, ON

- http://www.northernc.on.ca/net-11/edkirk/curator/curator.htm
- http://www.northernc.on.ca/museum/

Early life in Kirkland Lake and Northeast Ontario is portrayed in the former home of prospector and multi-millionaire Harry Oakes, as well as the millionaire lifestyle and local hockey heroes.

Sir John Johnson House National Historic Site – Prescott, ON
[English & French]
http://parkscanada.pch.gc.ca/parks/ontario/j_johnson_house/j_johnson_housee.htm
The former home of the famous Loyalist.

South Grey Museum and Historical Library – Flesherton, ON
http://www.greycounty.on.ca/museum/sgmusfpg.html
Features exhibits and archival material focusing on the people of South East Grey County.

South Simcoe Pioneer Museum – Alliston, New Tecumseth, ON
http://susan.chin.gc.ca:8016/BASIS/guide/user/search/DDW?M=1&U=1&W=GUIDE_KEY=1456
Presents local history, including transportation and agriculture, in a log cabin and English barn.

Southwold Earthworks National Historic Site – Leamington, ON [English & French]
http://parkscanada.pch.gc.ca/parks/ontario/southwold_earthworks/southwold_earthworkse.htm
The site of a former Attiwandaronk village from around 1500 AD.

Thunder Bay Museum – Thunder Bay, ON
http://www.tbaytel.net/tbhms/
Exhibits featuring displays of native peoples, the fur trade, police and Northern Ontario history.

Timmins Museum: National Exhibition Centre – South Porcupine, ON
http://susan.chin.gc.ca:8016/BASIS/guide/user/search/DDW?M=1&U=1&W=GUIDE_KEY=1076
Exhibits depicting the history of the Porcupine Gold Rush and pioneers of New Ontario.

Todmorden Mills Heritage Museum and Arts Centre – East York, ON
http://www.metrotor.on.ca/services/parks/parks/todmo.html
This East York community museum features costumed interpreters at the site of former saw mill, paper mill, grist mill, brewery and distillery. Also features the Don River Railway station.

Toronto Historical Board – Toronto, ON
http://www.torontohistory.on.ca/history/history.html
This Web site contains information on several museums and historic sites in the city of Toronto. Attractions included are Historic Fort York, Colborne Lodge, The Spadina House and Gardens, Mackenzie House, and 205 Yonge St., the THB Resource Center.

Toronto's First Post Office – Toronto, ON
http://www.web-sights.com/tfpo/
The only Canadian postal museum depicting pre-Confederation British North American postal history. Houses an extensive collection of postal artifacts and research archives.

Toronto – Tollkeeper's Cottage Project
http://www.geocities.com/Heartland/Meadows/2271/
Details of efforts to save this historic cottage on the corner of Bathurst and Davenport.

Trent-Severn Waterway National Historic Site – Trenton to Port Severn, ON [English & French]
http://parkscanada.pch.gc.ca/parks/ontario/trent-sev-waterway/trent-sev-waterwaye.htm
An online tour, history and photos of this 386-km waterway that served the native peoples of central Ontario as well as the lumber and agriculture industries and recreational boating.

Upper Canada Village - Morrisburg, ON
http://www.parks.on.ca/uc.village/index.html
This living history museum features costumed interpreters in an 1860's village, complete with shops, artisans, churches, homes and farms, located along the St. Lawrence River.

Uxbridge-Scott Museum – Uxbridge, ON
http://www.uxbridge.com/museum/mhome.html
Historic buildings and artifacts presenting the Quaker heritage of Uxbridge Township and area.

Watson's Mill/Dickinson Square Conservation Area – Manotick, ON
http://www3.sympatico.ca/rideauca/dickin1.html
A working 19th-century grist mill at the heart of an historic square and local shops.

Wellington County Museum and Archives – Fergus, ON
- http://www.freespace.net/community/centre/county/museum.html
- http://www.iosphere.net/~jholwell/cangene/wel-mus.html

Exhibits and archives recounting the county's social, agricultural, economic and cultural history.

Westfield Heritage Village – Rockton, ON
http://www.worldchat.com/public/westfield/westf1.htm
A living history museum with over 30 heritage buildings in a 324-acre natural park. The Web site offers a "virtual walking tour" of the entire village.

West Parry Sound District Museum – Parry Sound, ON
http://www.zeuter.com/~wpschin/
Several permanent and temporary exhibits and events celebrating the culture of the North.

Windsor's Community Museum/François Baby House – Windsor, ON
http://www.city.windsor.on.ca/wpl/museum/
Exhibits depicting the individuals, cultures and events that contributed to Windsor's history.

Woodside National Historic Site – Kitchener, ON [English & French]
http://parkscanada.pch.gc.ca/parks/ontario/woodside/woodsidee.htm
The 1890's restored boyhood home of Prime Minister William Lyons Mackenzie King. Take an online tour of the home, read about its history or view photos of Woodside.

Woodstock Museum – Woodstock, ON
http://www.city.woodstock.on.ca/admin_structure/comm_services/museum_artgallery.htm
Eight exhibits in the former town hall depicting Woodstock history from 10,000 BC to 2001.

Professional Organization

Ontario Museum Association
http://www.museumassn.on.ca/
Open to individual or institutional members, the OMA promotes the awareness and preservation of Ontario's heritage with professional development, government advocacy and publications.

Military, Native and Historic Groups

31 Names From a WWI Autograph Book
http://www.globalgenealogy.com/LCGS/M-AGRAF.HTM
A transcription of an autograph book from Perth, ON, with names of Ontario soldiers.

Links to Your Canadian Past

Ontario and the Western Provinces

42nd Pipes and Drums of Lanark & Renfrew
http://www.ravnwood.com/music/42nd/index.htm
Includes a history emigration to Ontario and this unit, which began as the Brockford Battalion.

48th Highlanders Old Comrades Association
http://www.rose.com/~ronk/
Dedicated to preserving the history of this military regiment.

Butler's Rangers
http://iaw.on.ca/~awoolley/brang/brang.html
Many links to information and images of this unit headquartered at Fort Niagara 1777-84.

Cameron Highlanders of Ottawa
http://www.geocities.com/Area51/9252/chofo.htm
Includes origins and history of the regiment, with honors, battles and insignia.

Essex Scottish Regiment – "Oh Canada We Stand Guard for Thee"
http://webhome.idirect.com/~wtcook/tribute.html
Includes an historical background and modern history of the regiment.

Hastings County, Midland District Upper Canada Militia Roll 1818
http://www.iwaynet.net/~bobphillips/muster.htm
Includes e-mail links to descendants, where known.

Index to Ontario Loyalists
http://www.rootsweb.com/~ote/indexloy.htm#ontario
Many links to varied information on loyalists, plus several regiment and muster lists.

International Order of Oddfellows: History of the Ontario Order
http://norm28.hsc.usc.edu/IOOF/Canada/OntarioHistory.html
Describes the development of the movement in the province of Ontario.

King's Rangers [English & French]
http://www.cam.org/~dmonk/
The history of this British regiment, many of whom settled in Ontario after 1784.

Lanark County Names on a WWII Plaque in Bar River
http://www.globalgenealogy.com/LCGS/M-BAR.HTM
Transcription of an old (unidentified) newspaper clipping describing the plaque, with names.

Lincoln and Welland Regiment: History
http://www.iaw.on.ca/~awoolley/lincweld.html
History and photos of this reserve infantry unit of the Canadian Forces.

Living History in Thunder Bay
http://loon.norlink.net/~jkeigher/
Includes links to several military re-enactment groups in the area, including the Canadian Corps of Voyageurs and the HM Regiment DeMeuron.

London and Middlesex County Honour Rolls
- **World War I**: http://discover.lpl.london.on.ca/bkshelf/spotlite/forget/1914.htm
- **World War II**: http://discover.lpl.london.on.ca/bkshelf/spotlite/forget/ww2lon.htm

London Home Guard 1866
http://www.rootsweb.com/~onmiddle/HomeGuard.html
A list of men sworn in in June 1866 to constitute the city's home guard.

Lorne Scots Enrollment – World War II
http://www.hhpl.on.ca/localhistory/lornescots.htm
A searchable index to the local military regiment from Halton and Peel.

Métis Nation of Ontario
http://www.metisnation.org/
Includes sections on History and Culture, Women of the Métis Nation of Ontario, Métis Youth, Training Initiatives, Scholarships and Bursaries and the newsletter *Métis Voyageur*.

North Bay Honour Roll
http://www.city.north-bay.on.ca/nblegion/index.htm
Names of local individuals who served in World Wars I & II, the Korean and Gulf Wars.

Ontario Métis Aboriginal Association
http://www.omaa.org/
"OMAA is the Representative Assembly which serves to protect, promote, and enhance the social, cultural, and political aspirations of the Métis and those Indian people not residing on reserves in Ontario."

The Queen's Own Rifles of Canada
http://www.qor.com/
The history and current status of this regiment, stationed in Toronto.

The Queen's York Rangers
http://www.connection.com/~qyrang/
Information on the 1st American Regiment of the Royal Canadian Armoured Corps.

Renfrew – First World War Veterans and Casualties from Renfrew, Ontario
http://www.archives.ca/db/cef/memorial.html
Part of the National Archives of Canada, this site contains an index of soldiers who served in the Canadian Expeditionary Force, with scanned copies of attestation papers.

Reserve Militia Company Roll, 1871
http://www.globalgenealogy.com/LCGS/LCGSMIL.HTM
A list of 508 men from Lanark Village, Lanark Township and Darling Township.

The Scout Brigade of Fort George
http://www.scout.net/~ftgeorge/
Observe or participate (as a British or American Soldier) in an historic re-enactment of the life of a soldier in 1812-13 at historic Fort George. Participants don mock uniforms and participate in battles, drills and parades on the second weekend after Canadian Labour Day each year.

Tribes and Bands of Ontario
http://hanksville.phast.umass.edu:8000/cultprop/contacts/tribal/ON.html
Addresses and contact information from tribal groups throughout the province.

United Empire Loyalists Association of Canada

- **London & Western Ontario Branch**: http://www.multiboard.com/~spettit/lwouel.html
- **Niagara Branch**: http://www.npiec.on.ca/~uela/cjb1.htm

War of 1812 Muster Rolls
http://www.rootsweb.com/~ote/1812mil.htm
Includes men under Major (then Colonel) Willocks, the Corps of Canadian Volunteers, Non-combatant prisoners of war and property losses from Newark and men who joined the enemy.

Widows Receiving Pensions from the War of 1812
http://www.rootsweb.com/~ote/1812ac.htm
Includes the soldier's name, rank and date and place of death.

William Jarvis and the Queen's Rangers
http://www.torontohistory.on.ca/jarvis/index.htm
A biography of Jarvis along with history and images of the Queen's Rangers.

Provincial and Local History and Photos

Provincial and Regional History and Photos

Amalgamation of Ontario Communities
http://www.globalgenealogy.com/LCGS/A-AMALG.HTM
Information on the provincial government's plan to reduce the number of municipalities by amalgamating existing towns. A table of amalgamated towns and links to official information.

Between Two Rivers: A Profile of the People and Places of the Upper Ottawa Valley
http://www.renc.igs.net/~ogrady/opeongo/
A look at the settlements along the Opeongo Line, Renfrew Valley and O'Grady Settlement, with a section on local expressions and individual communities.

Links to Your Canadian Past
Ontario and the Western Provinces

Canada West: Districts, Counties and Townships of 1846
http://www.rootsweb.com/~ote/1846dist.htm
Explains the early geographic divisions of what later became Ontario.

History of Ontario
http://www.rootsweb.com/~ote/onthist.htm
A brief timeline with major events in the province's history highlighted.

Human History in the Grand River Watershed
http://www.schoolnet.ca/collections/copper/low/humanhist.htm
Includes pages on Native People, European Settlement and Industry and Land Use and Problems.

Logging By Rail in Algonquin Park
http://www3.sympatico.ca/past.forward/video.htm
Description and selected text and photos from a 1930 video produced by the Fassett Lumber Corporation inside the park and in Fossmill in Chisholm Township.

Northwestern Ontario History
http://www.northwestinfo.com/regional/general_info/history.html
An informative sketch of how exploration, fur trading and silver mining affected the area.

Ontario: History [English & French]
http://www.gov.on.ca/MBS/english/its_ontario/ont-hist/index.html
A series of texts from the Government of Ontario covering the history of the province from native cultures through European settlement and clashes, the War of 1812, Confederation, etc.

Links to Your Canadian Past

Ontario and the Western Provinces

Ontario History
http://www.rootsweb.com/~canon/ontbegin.html
An overview of the political and territorial evolution of the province, with maps.

Rainy River District – 100 Years, 100 Stories: The History of the Rainy River District
http://www.schoolnet.ca/collections/frances/
A series of original articles and photos from the *Fort Frances Times* and *Rainy River Herald*, recounting the gold rush, logging industry, railways and highways in the area's development.

Rideau Canal Waterway
- **Human History**: http://www.rideau-info.com/canal/human_history.html
- **Canal History**: http://www.rideau-info.com/canal/history.html

Spirits of the Little Bonnechere: A History of Exploration, Logging and Settlement, 1800-1920
http://www.fcbe.edu.on.ca/~mackayr/spiritbk.htm
Excerpts and several photos from a book by the same name about the Bonnechere River.

A "Wee" Bit of Townships History
http://www.intranet.ca/deepriver/shistory.html
Historical facts on the townships and industries of the United Townships of Alice, Rolph, Buchanan, Wylie, McKay and Petawawa.

Cultural Groups

Black History in Guelph and Wellington County
http://www.museum.guelph.on.ca/bl2.htm
This online exhibit of Guelph Museums is comprehensive, dealing with slavery, the Underground Railroad, Black settlements, Religion, Family Histories and other aspects of Black History.

Links to Your Canadian Past
Ontario and the Western Provinces

Black History in Southwestern Ontario
- http://www.ciaccess.com/~jdnewby/kent.htm
- http://www.ciaccess.com/~jdnewby/morehistory.htm

Includes biographical information on prominent Black citizens, as well as information on Black schools and churches in Chatham. Second page: Information on the Elgin settlement.

Croatians in Canada and Ontario
http://www.dalmatia.net/croatia/emmigrants/cro-can.htm
A detailed and very informative account of the story of Croatian emigration to the province.

A **Historical Sketch of the Brethren in Christ Church, Known as Tunkers in Canada**
http://www.easynet.ca/~johnb/tunkers/
The complete text of a book about the Mennonite church in Markham, with information on families from the Bertie, Bethesda, Clarence, Howick, Nottawa, Springvale, Wainfleet and Waterloo District churches.

Icelandic History and Settlement
http://web.idirect.com/~icct/articles.html
Articles on Icelanders in Kinmount and the province of Ontario and Aoalstein's visit to Ontario.

History of the Catholic Church in Waterloo County
http://www.planetc.com/users/spetzj/spetzinfo/family_pictures/pics_from_old_book/xi.htm
The entire text of a published history of the Catholic Church in the county, with illustrations.

Slave, Soldier, Settler: One Pioneer's Story, The Life of Richard Pierpoint
http://www.baxter.net/edunet/cat/pioneer.html
The extraordinary life of this individual is recounted from birth in Senegal to a slave market in the U.S. to fighting in Butler's Rangers and receiving a land grant in Ontario.

Local History and Photos

Almonte History
http://www.almonte.com/history.html
Describes the settlement, development of the wool industry and name of the town.

Arnprior (Renfrew County) – A Brief History of Arnprior
http://www.magma.ca/~gacc/history.htm

Bracebridge History
http://www.town.bracebridge.on.ca/history.html
Includes photos and an article on the town's heritage and a capsule history of Bracebridge.

Brant County History
http://www.worldchat.com/public/cplace/brahist.htm
Overview of the county's development, and the histories of individual communities.

Brantford History
http://www.city.brantford.on.ca/tourism/josephbrant.html
Recounts the life of Joseph Brant (Thayendanegea) and the naming and founding of the town.

Bruce County – History of Bruce County From a Genealogical Focus
http://www.compunik.com/vmall/bcgs/bcgshist.htm
Includes a map of municipalities in the county, a list of defunct towns and name changes.

Burlington Photograph Collection
http://www.hhpl.on.ca/localhistory/bplphotos.htm
Search 2,000 photos from the Ivan Cleaver Postcard Collection and Burlington Historical Society Photograph Collection.

Calvin (Nipissing District) – A History of Calvin Township
http://tnt.vianet.on.ca/community/genweb/calvin.htm
Taken from the book *Calvin Remembers One Hundred Years, 1887 - 1987* by Richard Gould.

Carleton Place – A Short History of Carleton Place
http://www.town.carleton-place.on.ca/HISTORY.HTM
From its settlement to avert the threat of American invasion, through industry, to today.

Chatham's History [same page at both sites]
- http://www.city.chatham-kent.on.ca/chatham/history.htm
- http://www.wincom.net/CHATHAM/history.htm

A good amount of information is packed into this overview of the town's history.

Cobourg – A Brief History of Cobourg
http://www.town.cobourg.on.ca/tourism/history.html
Two hundred years of Cobourg history, since its founding by United Empire Loyalists.

Cumberland's History
http://www.municipality.cumberland.on.ca/en/welcome.html
A brief overview of the city's past, including Orléans and the municipal symbols.

Darling – The French Settlement in Darling Township
http://www.globalgenealogy.com/LCGS/A-FR.HTM
A brief but interesting article on the Francophone history of this town by a descendant.

Essex County History
http://www.rootsweb.com/~onessex/ehis.htm
A timeline/list of historical and anecdotal information about the county's development.

Essex County Farm Life
http://www.geocities.com/Heartland/Hills/6401/joyce.html
Text of a presentation given by the granddaughter of local settlers for Museum Heritage Week.

Flesherton History
http://www.greycounty.on.ca/museum/sgmhist.html
A short text on W.K. Flesher, who founded and lent his name to this town.

Galt- History of the City of Galt
http://www.city.cambridge.on.ca/profile/history/galt.html

Grey County/Owen Sound Historic Photographs
http://www.greycounty.on.ca/museum/hphoto.html
Dozens of historical images from the collection of the County of Grey-Owen Sound Museum.

Guelph's Heritage: A Walking Tour of the Downtown Core
http://www.uoguelph.ca/history/urban/tour.html
Includes an introduction to the city's history and founder John Galt.

Guelph – Henry Langley and the Making of Gothic Guelph
http://www.uoguelph.ca/history/urban/article3.html
This scholarly article examines the role of the Toronto architect in the city's architecture.

Halton County Historical Overview
http://www.hhpl.on.ca/sigs/genweb/haltonsketches.htm
A reprinted article from John McDonald's book *Halton Sketches Revisited: Historical Tales of People and Events in North Halton.*

Halton County Local Community Histories
HTTP://www.hhpl.on.ca/sigs/ehs/comm.html
Links to detailed histories with historic photographs of several towns in the county.

Halton Hills Photograph Collection
http://www.hhpl.on.ca/localhistory/hhplphotos.htm
A searchable database of over 4,000 historic photos from the Esquesing Historical Society.

Hamilton – A History of Hamilton
http://www.city.hamilton.on.ca/handbook/histofha.htm
A series of short articles from La Salle and Loyalists through industrial and regional growth.

Hamilton-Wentworth Region Trivia
http://www.hamilton-went.on.ca/trivia.htm
Includes Historical Trivia, Hamilton-Wentworth Firsts, Notable Dates and Strange But True.

Hamilton – A Brief History of the Custom House
http://www.web.net/~owahc/1332.htm
The story of this historic building and its many roles and uses since 1855.

Hespeler – History of the Town of Hespeler
http://www.city.cambridge.on.ca/profile/history/hespeler.html

Huron County Townships
http://www.geocities.com/Heartland/Meadows/8965/townships.html
Town histories and information from *The Settlement of Huron County*, by James Scott (1966).

Kapuskasing – Municipalité de Kapuskasing : Histoire
http://www.intergov.gc.ca/mun/on/kap/histoirf.html
A brief history of this northern Ontario town once known as MacPherson.

Kent County History
http://www.rootsweb.com/~onessex/khis.htm
A timeline of major events in the development of the county.

King Township History
http://www.township.king.on.ca/tokhist.htm#History
A brief history of the township, including the communities of Kettleby and Schomberg.

Kingston – Greater Kingston, Ontario [English & French]
http://www.acpo.on.ca/claude/kingst-a.htm
A map of the area and brief history of Kingston and surrounding townships.

Kingston and Pembroke Railway
http://www.globalserve.net/~robkath/railkrp.htm
A brief history of this important rail line in Eastern Ontario and what remains of it today.

Kitchener – "From Berlin to Kitchener"
http://www.lib.uwaterloo.ca/tour/Berlin/Berlin.html
Textual excerpts and images from the diaries of two brothers dealing with the debate over the changing of the town's name in 1916.

Lakefield Historical Notes
http://www.lakefield-district.com/history.htm
Focusing on the role of the Trent-Severn Waterway in the town's settlement and growth.

Lanark County History
http://www.county.lanark.on.ca/histpage.htm
Links to articles on early settlers, the Rideau Canal, the late 19th and early 20th centuries.

London Heritage Stories
http://www.fanshawec.on.ca/~Debra/historical/stories/stories.htm
Several articles on pioneers, notable citizens, historic locations and London's first dog.

London – Milestones in London Transit History
http://www.fanshawec.on.ca/~Debra/historical/ltc/Mstones.htm
A timeline of 123 years of transportation history, beginning in 1873.

Long Point Settlement Chronology
http://alpha.nornet.on.ca/~jcardiff/settlers/lspchronology.htm
A detailed timeline of the period 1790-1796. In progress.

Mattawa (Nipissing District) – Mattawa History and Facts
http://www.city.north-bay.on.ca/mattawa/mw-facts.htm
An overview of the important events in the settlement, development and history of Mattawa.

Merrickville – The Founding of Merrickville/ History of the Township of Wolford
http://www3.sympatico.ca/merrickville/PAST.HTM
The separate, brief histories of these two towns, amalgamated on 1 January, 1998.

Middlesex County History
http://www.rootsweb.com/~onmiddle/onthistory.html
A timeline of the changing landscape and borders of the county from 1788 to 1865.

Nancy Island – A Piece of History
http://www.waynecook.com/rose.html
An article by Marilyn Beecroft of Wasaga Beach Provincial Park on how Nancy Island got its name from a British supply ship used in the War of 1812.

Nepean History
- http://www.city.nepean.on.ca/communit/history.htm
- http://www.ncf.carleton.ca/ip/government/nepean/about/history

An introduction to the town's past and namesake Sir Evan Nepean. The second link is a text-only account of the city's history and relationship with Ottawa.

Norfolk County – "Glorious Old Norfolk"
http://alpha.nornet.on.ca/~jcardiff/media/oldboys/glorious.htm
A long series of articles on first explorers and settlers and individual town histories.

Norfolk County Photos and Bios
http://alpha.nornet.on.ca/~jcardiff/media/oldboys/photos.htm
Information and images from the out-of-print book *Simcoe and Norfolk County.*

Norfolk County History
http://www.rootsweb.com/~canon/norfolk/history.html
A timeline of the various changes in the geography and borders of the county.

North Bay
- **History**: http://www.city.north-bay.on.ca/history/history.htm
- **Historic Photographs**: http://www.city.north-bay.on.ca/museum/napics01.htm
- **Local Architecture**: http://www.city.north-bay.on.ca/museum/fanala~1.htm

North Gower: The Way We Were
http://magi.com/~longpath/wewere.htm
A series of brief articles and photos of local places and historic sites and events.

Oakville History
http://www.oakvilleonline.com/history.htm
A comprehensive overview of the town's history, with links to further information on aspects of the town's history and prominent citizens. More links to other historical articles on the town.

Otonabee – The Settling of Otonabee Township in Peterborough County
http://www.peterboro.net/~resson/marion.htm
Includes a list of early industries and the history of the villages of Keene and Lang.

Ottawa – History of Canada's Capital Region
http://www.capcan.ca/english/about/historic/history_ncr.html
Sections on aboriginal peoples, fur trade and settlement, economic and political development.

Parry Sound – History of Parry Sound
http://www.parrysound.com/History/history.html

Perth County Name Origins and Changes
http://www.rootsweb.com/~onperth/places.html
Brief information on the origins and changes in the names of townships and communities.

Petawawa Township (Renfrew County): A View of the Valley
http://www.valleynet.on.ca/~aa127/uovgen/renfrew/History/petawawa.html
A brief overview of the town's place in the county, its settlement and development.

Peterborough County History
http://www.county.peterborough.on.ca/history.htm

Peterborough: Then and Now
http://www.kawartha.net/~jleonard/thennow.htm
Juxtaposed photographs of old and present-day Peterborough tell the story of change in the town.

Prescott-Russell Counties – The Forgotten Wharves of the United Counties of Prescott-Russell
http://www.cyberus.ca/~jlpilon/jeanfr.htm
History and photos of early commercial navigation, wharf construction and individual townships.

Preston – History of the Town of Preston
http://www.city.cambridge.on.ca/profile/history/preston.html
From early Mennonite and German-speaking settlers through the mineral springs to today.

Ridgetown – The History of Ridgetown, Ontario, Canada
- http://205.207.151.2:80/ridgetown/hist.htm
- http://city.chatham-kent.on.ca/ridgetown/history.htm

A detailed overview of the history of the town from First Nations settlement to the early 1900's.

St. Marys – Historical Background of the Grand Trunk Railway
http://stonetown.com/gttsm/history.htm
This article gives the intertwined history of the town of Saint Mary's and the extension of the Grand Trunk Railway through this part of Ontario.

Sault Ste. Marie: A Community's History Through the Prism of Its Heritage Sites
http://www.schoolnet.ca/collections/ssm/pages/english/home.html
An excellent visual and textual presentation of the town's rich history.

Scott Township History
http://www.uxbridge.com/town/scott.html
A brief overview from 1807-1973, when parts of Scott were amalgamated into Uxbridge.

Simcoe County Townships
http://www.rootsweb.com/~ote/simcoe/index.htm
Includes a list and historical anecdotes of current and former townships in the county.

Simcoe County History
http://www.genweb.net/~simcoe/history.html

Stormont, Dundas and Glengarry Historical Society Historic Photo Collection
http://www.cnwl.igs.net/~slm/photgall.htm

Timmins, Ontario History
http://www.city.timmins.on.ca/community/comm.htm

Toronto – A Short History of Toronto
http://www.torontohistory.on.ca/archives/shorthistory.html
Lots of information packed into a short textual overview of the city's history.

Toronto – "How Was the Town of York Founded?"
http://www.torontohistory.on.ca/archives/york.html

Toronto – A History of Fort York
http://www.torontohistory.on.ca/archives/guide.html
From its founding in 1793 by John Graves Simcoe to the War of 1812 and restoration.

Toronto History Page
http://www.trannamedia.com/history/
Sections include People and Places, Historical Events and Maps and Other Resources.

Toronto Harbour Chart History
http://csx.cciw.ca/dfo/chs/edu/harbour-history.html
Focusing on the 1792 hydrographic survey of Toronto by Joseph Bouchette.

Uxbridge – The Founding of Uxbridge
http://www.uxbridge.com/town/uxhist.html
An overview from survey to settlement and growth from hamlet to village, town and municipality.

Uxbridge Quaker Heritage
http://www.uxbridge.com/heritage/quakers.html
Covers the roots of Uxbridge Quakerism, Quaker Beliefs and the founding of Uxbridge.

Vanier – Municipalité de Vanier: Histoire [French only]
http://www.intergov.gc.ca/mun/on/vanier/histoirf.html
A (very) brief history of this town, formerly known as Cummings Island, Janeville and Eastview.

Victoria County

- **Early Settlement**: http://www.angelfire.com/ms/SkeletonsintheCloset/SETTLEMENT.html
- **Individual townships**: http://members.tripod.com/~VictoriaCounty/Settlement.html
- **Photos**: http://members.tripod.com/~VictoriaCounty/Pictures.html

Waterloo Historical Outline
http://dcs1.uwaterloo.ca/~marj/history/whs.html
An informative overview of Waterloo's history from the 18th century to the present.

West Carleton: An Historical Perspective
http://twp.west-carleton.on.ca/history.htm
Brief histories of the amalgamated townships of Torbolton, Huntley and Fitzroy.

Wolford – The History of the Township of Wolford
See Merrickvile, above. Wolford and Merrickville were amalgamated on 1 January, 1998.

Family Associations / Surnames

Province-wide and Regional Surnames

Bruce County Genealogical Society
- **Queries**: http://www.compunik.com/vmall/bcgs/bcgsquer.htm
- **Surname Interests**: http://www.compunik.com/vmall/bcgs/bcgssurn.htm

Conrad Grebel College Mennonite Genealogies
http://www.lib.uwaterloo.ca/MHSC/gen5.html

Erin Township (Wellington County) Biographies
http://www.chelmsford.com/home/priestner/bios.htm
Biographies of John McLean and Alexander and Hugh McMillan.

Essex County – Pioneer Families of Essex County and the Detroit River Region
http://www.rootsweb.com/~onessex/pioneers.htm
Historical dates and anecdotes about early settlers, beginning in the early 1700's.

Glengarry County Family Trees/Histories
http://members.tripod.com/~GLENGARRY/FamilyTrees.html
Information on what families are included varies from time to time.

Haliburton County Pioneer Families
http://www.cancom.net/~cmiles/pioneer.html
Information of varying length on early settlers in the county.

Links to Your Canadian Past
Ontario and the Western Provinces

Kent County Pioneers
http://www.rootsweb.com/~onessex/kentpion.htm
A list of early settlers, with the date they arrived or were born, and their profession.

Lanark County Genealogy Society

- **Family Histories**:
  http://www.globalgenealogy.com/LCGS/LCGSDOCS.HTM#HISTS
- **Queries**:
  http://www.globalgenealogy.com/LCGS/LCGSQURY.HTM

Leeds and Grenville Genealogy Society Query Page
http://www.cybertap.com/genealogy/page9.html

Lennox and Addington Museum and Archives Family Files
http://fox.nstn.ca/~museum/geneol.html

Malahide Township Queries
http://www.ptbruce.kanservu.ca/Genealogy/queries.html

Norfolk County Pioneer Families
http://www.rootsweb.com/~canon/norfolk/families.html
Biographical sketches of families who settled in the area prior to 1860, with descendant contacts.

Norfolk Historical Society Family Histories
http://alpha.nornet.on.ca/~jcardiff/resources/familyhistories.htm

Northumberland County Pioneer Families
http://www.geocities.com/Heartland/Meadows/3807/ontgen/frstfam.html
Biographical sketches for families who settled in Northumberland towns before 1860.

Links to Your Canadian Past
Ontario and the Western Provinces

Ontario GenWeb

- **Prominent People and Families**: http://www.rootsweb.com/~canon/prominen.html
- **Queries**: http://www.rootsweb.com/~canon/ontquery.html
- **Surname Interests**: http://www.rootsweb.com/~canon/prominen.html

Oxford County Early Settlers and Pioneers
http://www.geocities.com/Heartland/Acres/7990/Oxford_Settlers.html
An alphabetical index to excerpted information on people in the county prior to 1860.

Perth County – Historical Sketches of Perth County Pioneers
http://www.rootsweb.com/~onperth/sketches.html
Excerpted biographical information from *History of the County of Perth from 1825 to 1902.*

Renfrew – Heritage Renfrew: Family Names Traced Using Our Facilities
http://www.renc.igs.net/~renarch/#BANK

Temiskaming Genealogy Group Surname Interests
http://www.nt.net/~timetrav/table.html

Uxbridge – In Search of Family Records in Uxbridge, Ontario
http://www.uxbridge.com/search/fr_names.html
Click on a family name in the left column to view queries/information.

Victoria County

- **Influential Men**: http://members.tripod.com/~VictoriaCounty/Biography.html
- **Pioneers** (by township): http://members.tripod.com/~VictoriaCounty/Pioneers.html

Links to Your Canadian Past
Ontario and the Western Provinces

Waterloo Genealogical Cooperative
http://hometown.aol.com/ernm/roots/waterloo.html
A list of homepages of those researching surnames and families in the Waterloo area.

York County Families
http://www.rootsweb.com/~onyork/ycf.html
Links to individuals with home pages of particular interest to York County family historians.

Individual Surnames or Family Associations

Banks: http://www3.sk.sympatico.ca/shelley/gene/banksbk.html

Baxter: http://www3.sk.sympatico.ca/baxlev/

Becker: http://www.familytreemaker.com/users/b/a/k/Jeffrey--Baker/COL2-0001.html

Burger: http://www.bond.net/~dburger/lore001.htm

Burns: http://www3.sympatico.ca/ag.lewis/history.htm

Carney: http://www.onlink.net/~dcarney/RC1/WC_TOC.htm

Collinson: http://www.pathcom.com/~carolron/family.htm

Cook: http://www.waynecook.com/cook.html

Danert: http://www.familytreemaker.com/users/m/c/a/Marjorie-K-McArthur/ODT19-0001.html

Doersam (Waterloo County): http://users.sisna.com/doersam/

Donnelly: http://www.lonet.ca/res/donnelly/donnelly.html

Dracup: http://www.king.igs.net/~gregg/dracup2.htm

Eby (Aebi): http://www.familytreemaker.com/users/q/u/a/B-D-Quast/GENE1-0004.html

Erb:
http://www.geocities.com/Heartland/Pointe/4085/ontario.html

Esson: http://www.peterboro.net/~resson/ron.htm

Fraser:
http://www.geocities.com/Heartland/Prairie/9943/genealogy.html

Gellatly: http://marlo.eagle.ca/~douggell/gellatly.html

Gidley: http://www.geocities.com/Heartland/Estates/4294/

Girling: http://www.mystic.mb.ca/mvickers/girling/index.html

Hagerman: http://www.geocities.com/Heartland/Ranch/8401/

Hampel:
http://www.freenet.hamilton.on.ca/~ab501/Gen/Surnames/Hampel/hampel.html

The Harris Family:
http://www.fanshawec.on.ca/~Debra/historical/stories/harris.htm
This brief article describes the life of John and Amelia Harris, who lived in the Eldon House in London in the 1830's and 40's.

Hinton: http://home.att.net/~ramosgang/Hinton.html

Holme: http://webination.com/holmes/

Homeyer:
http://www.geocities.com/Heartland/Plains/7764/homelist.html

Kipp: http://www2.magmacom.com/~ekipp/

Kirkwood: http://www.igs.net/~vkirkwoodhp/kirk2.htm

Langedijk:
http://www.geocities.com/Heartland/Acres/7241/index.html

Luesby: http://home.interhop.net/~rmacleod/luesby.htm

MacLean Clan:
http://ourworld.compuserve.com/homepages/donmac/

Maguire: http://users.uniserve.com/~makyta/welcome.html [very comprehensive]

Marlatt, Malott, Mellott:
http://members.aol.com/BMarlatt/homepage.html

Marshall:
http://www.geocities.com/Heartland/Plains/7525/Marshall/marshal l.htm

McCabe: http://www.mccabeclan.com/families.htm

McCarthy: http://www3.sympatico.ca/djmccarthy/index.html

McKane: http://www.mckane.waterloo.on.ca/geneal/

McKenzie: http://www.swanvalley.freenet.mb.ca/~gwmckenz/

McLaren:
http://www.familytreemaker.com/users/m/c/l/Lawrence-L-McLaren/index.html

Mulcaster:
http://www.geocities.com/Heartland/Hills/6401/contents.html

O'Grady: http://www.renc.igs.net/~ogrady/opeongo/reg104.html

Ouimet: http://www.geocities.com/~couimet/lehouymet.html [English & French]

Parker: http://www3.sympatico.ca/djmccarthy/index.html#Parker

Pegg: http://www.geocities.com/Heartland/Meadows/8035/

Pilgrim: http://www.cyberus.ca/~pmarchan/pilgene.htm

Renaud: http://www.geocities.com/Heartland/Meadows/6257/

Rodrigue:
http://www.genealogie.org/famille/rodrigue/rodrigue.html

Strong: http://home.netinc.ca/~wstrong/strong1.htm

Summers: http://home.att.net/~ramosgang/Summers.html

Thompson: http://home.ica.net/~runesmith/gene/thompson.html

Truax/du Trieux: http://home.ica.net/~runesmith/gene/truax.html

Uttley: http://www.geocities.com/SouthBeach/7109/uttley.html

Valleau: http://www.geocities.com/Heartland/Prairie/1181/

Vance: http://www.execulink.com/~johnb/VanceGeneology.htm

Van Normand: http://www.multiboard.com/~spettit/vnfa/

Vine: http://www.library.elgin-county.on.ca/~frank/Hist16-1.html

Waylett: http://www.familytreemaker.com/users/w/a/y/Douglas--C-Waylett/ODT2-0005.html

Weston:
http://www.geocities.com/Athens/Forum/6500/weston.htm

Wilson: http://www.bigwave.ca/~john/wilson.html

Chat Rooms and Mailing Lists

Ontario Mailing List: majordomo@listserv.northwest.com
all: subscribe ontario;
digest: subscribe ontario-digest

Ontario Mailing List (Rootsweb)
all: ontario-l-request@rootsweb.com;
digest: ontario-d-request@rootsweb.com

Ontario-Canada Mailing List (family history):
maiser@rmgate.pop.indiana.edu
sub ONTARIO-CANADA

Ontario Genealogical Society/International Genealogical Association Mailing List: listserv@hatlane.nosub iga_ogs

Ontario GenWeb
- **Chat Forum**: http://www.rootsweb.com/~canon/chat.html
- **Mailing List**:
  http://www.multiboard.com/~spettit/ongenweb/ogwmlist.html

Ontario Museum Mailing List (ONMUSE-L)
http://www.museumassn.on.ca/onmuse.htm

Ontarioan Genealogy Discussion List
http://www.links2go.com/froup/Ontarioan_Genealogy
A forum for discussion genealogy in Ontario, by Links2Go.

Durham County Mailing List (ONDURHAM)
all: ondurham-l-request@rootsweb.com;
digest: ondurham-d-request@rootsweb.com

Eastern Ontario Mailing List (EONTGEN-L)
http://www.ikweb.com/murduck/genealogy/eontgen-l/intro.htm

Essex County Mailing List: majordomo@listserv.northwest.com
Subscribe Essex County

Loyalists-in-Canada Mailing List:
majordomo@listserv.northwest.com
all: subscribe loyalists-in-canada;
digest: subscribe loyalists-in-canada-digest

Niagara-Ontario Mailing List
all: niagara-ont-l-request@rootsweb.com;
digest: niagara-ont-l-request@rootsweb.com

Upper Ottawa Valley Genealogy Mailing List (UOVGEN)
http://www.valleynet.on.ca/~aa127/uovgen/uovgen.html

Victoria County Mailing List
http://www.onelist.com/subscribe.cgi/VictoriaCounty

Saskatchewan

Genealogical, Historical and Cultural Societies

L'Association Culturelle (Catholique) Franco-Canadienne de la Saskatchewan [French only]
http://www.schoolnet.ca/collections/fransaskois/Associations/ACFC/acfc1.htm
Dedicated to promoting the interests and protecting and defending the rights of the French-speaking population of Saskatchewan.

Canadian Aviation Historical Society, Roland Groome Chapter – Regina, SK
http://www.gpfn.sk.ca/culture/history/cah.html
Contact, membership and newsletter information, along with Saskatchewan aviation "firsts."

The Francophone Community of Saskatchewan [English & French]
http://www.schoolnet.ca/collections/fransaskois/english.html
Information on the Education, Culture, Economy, Associations, Activities and other aspects of the French-speaking population of Saskatchewan.

Icelandic Club of Saskatchewan – Vatnabyggð
http://users.imag.net/~sry.rasgeirs/Elfros/VatNews.html
The online newsletter of the society, packed with information on projects, events, meetings, etc.

Links to Your Canadian Past

Ontario and the Western Provinces

Jewish Genealogical Exploration Guide for Manitoba and Saskatchewan (J-GEMS)
http://www.concentric.net/~Lkessler/jgems.shtml
A reference guide for Jewish genealogists in these two provinces, covering materials available, resource centers, a surname index and table of contents to all articles.

Saskatchewan Genealogical Society
http://www.saskgenealogy.com/
Information on the society, membership, branch contacts, major and special holdings of the library and how to make research requests. An index of the quarterly *Bulletin* is also provided, as is a provincial cemetery index and free queries, with results.

Saskatchewan GenWeb Project:
http://home.cc.umanitoba.ca/~umluther/uelac_manitoba/
Links to genealogical information, most of it indexed elsewhere in this volume.

- **Battleford Region**: http://www.rootsweb.com/~skbattle/Battleford/
- **Moose Jaw Region**: http://www.rootsweb.com/~skmoosej/MooseJaw/
- **Regina Region**: http://www.rootsweb.com/~skregina/Regina/
- **Saskatoon Region**: http://www.rootsweb.com/~sksaskat/Saskatoon/
- **Swift Current Region**: http://www.rootsweb.com/~skswiftc/SwiftCurrent/
- **Weyburn Region**: http://www.rootsweb.com/~skweybur/Weyburn/
- **Yorkton Region**: http://www.rootsweb.com/~skyorkto/Yorkton/

Saskatoon Heritage Society
http://www.sfn.saskatoon.sk.ca/arts/heritage/
Very stark, but provides information on the society's membership, activities and events, as well as publications, walking tours designated and protected buildings and local heritage groups.

La Société Historique de la Saskatchewan [English & French]
http://www.dlcwest.com/~acfc/Associations/socihist/intro.html
Dedicated to studying and promoting the francophone history, heritage and genealogy of the French-speaking population of Saskatchewan.

Zichydorf Village Association
http://www.feefhs.org/zva/frg-zva.html
Part of the Federation of East European Family History Societies (FEEFHS), this online association provides a newsletter, surname database, census and village info from the Austro-Hungarian homeland of the Zichydorf colony near Regina.

Archives

Archive Centers

Diefenbaker Canada Centre Archives
http://www.usask.ca/diefenbaker/arch.html
Materials concern former Prime Minister Diefenbaker and his career, but also Canada-U.S. relations, native studies, environmental studies, northern development, social welfare programs, etc. An online finding aid is included on the site.

Saskatchewan Archives Board
http://www.gov.sk.ca/govt/archives/
Describes both the government and historical records holdings in the archives, as well as contact information, operating hours and the journal *Saskatchewan History*.

City of Saskatoon Archives
http://www.city.saskatoon.sk.ca/cityhall/clerk/archives/archives.htm
Describes the range and scope of records contained in the city archives, including an index of Fire Insurance Plans (maps) and a finding aid for the sous-fonds of City Clerk's office records from 1903-1987. E-mail inquiries accepted via this site.

United Church of Canada Archives Network – Saskatchewan Conference Archives
http://www.uccan.org/archives/saskatchewan.htm
Baptism, marriage, burial, membership and other records of the Methodist, Presbyterian, and Congregational Churches of SK before 1925 and of The United Church of Canada after 1925.

University of Saskatchewan Archives National Archives of Canada Access Site
http://www.usask.ca/archives/das.html
One of the de-centralized locations of the National Archives of Canada, the University of Saskatchewan access site allows researchers to conduct research at a distance thanks to a number of National Archives CD-ROM finding aids, including ArchiVia2 (government & private records), Aboriginal Peoples, Colonial Archives and Prime Ministers.

Professional Organization

Saskatchewan Council of Archives
http://www.usask.ca/archives/sca.html
The Council is a professional organization seeking to promote a cooperative provincial archive system with professional standards and practices. Membership, workshops and services provided are detailed, and copies of the Council's newsletter are available.

Libraries and Research Centers

Directories and Catalogs

HYTELNET Library Catalogues – Saskatchewan
http://moondog.usask.ca/hytelnet/ca0/SK.html
Links to telnet connections to provincial libraries, with instructions on how to connect.

Library Websites and Catalogues – Saskatchewan
http://www.nlc-bnc.ca/canlib/esask.htm
This site, provided by the National Library of Canada, is a listing links to the public, private and University libraries in the province with online information or catalogues.

Saskatchewan Province-wide Library Electronic Information System
http://www.lib.sk.ca/pleis/
A resource linking public libraries throughout the province. Includes SUNCAT, a provincial-wide library catalogue with over one million records, and an online virtual reference service.

Libraries and Research Centers

Regina Public Library – Prairie History Room
http://www.rpl.regina.sk.ca/about/services/prairie.shtml
A large collection of materials on Regina and Reginans, including local histories, books on the fur trade, Métis, local agriculture, immigration and biographies and family histories.

Saskatchewan Indian Cultural Centre
http://www.sicc.sk.ca/
The Centre seeks to maintain, revive and promote the traditions and cultural identity of the five Indian Cultures of the province – the Saulteux, Dakota, Assiniboine, Dene and Cree – through various cultural, educational and research programs. The site also provides access to searching their library catalogue via telnet and an online museum tour.

Saskatoon Public Library – Local History Room
http://www.publib.saskatoon.sk.ca/morrison_lhr.html
Information on the scope and holdings of the Local History Room in the Frances Morrison (Main) Branch of the Saskatoon Public Library. Provides hours and contact information, plus a link to searching the Public Access Catalogue via Telnet.

University of Regina Library
http://www.uregina.ca/~library/
This site provides general information about the library, plus information about the various collections, including the University Archives, Government Publications, Map Library and Special Collections, which focus on Saskatchewan and local history. The library's catalog is searchable through the site.

University of Saskatchewan History Department – Resources
http://www.usask.ca/history/deptresources.html
Links to information on the *Canadian Journal of History*, theses from 1912 to the present, occasional papers, the U of S historians' newsletter and bulletin of departmental events.

Birth, Marriage, Death, Census and Other Data Online

Vital Statistics and Parish Records

Saskatchewan Vital Records
http://www.familytreemaker.com/00000164.html
Where to write to obtain vital statistics records from the province of Saskatchewan.

Cemetery Information

Saskatchewan Cemetery Index
http://www.saskgenealogy.com/cemetery/cemetery.htm
Compiled and maintained by the Saskatchewan Genealogical Society, the index of approximately 3,000 burial sites is searchable by name or municipality, and provides a reference to the Saskatchewan Resident Index or LDS film number.

Benson – St. Joseph Catholic Cemetery
http://pixel.cs.vt.edu/library/cemeteries/canada/link/stjos.txt
Contains cemetery info, plus an index of burials with birth date and place, spouse or parents.

Bienfait Civic Cemetery

- http://cap.estevan.sk.ca/cemetery.records/bienfait/
  List of burials, compiled from site visits, town records and microfilmed obituaries.
- http://pixel.cs.vt.edu/library/cemeteries/canada/link/bienfait.txt
  An index of just the burials of Germans from Russia.

Denzil – St. Henry's Catholic Cemetery
http://www.rootsweb.com/~skstjose/sthenrys.html
An incomplete list of burials in this cemetery.

Estevan Cemetery Records
Compiled from on-site visits, town records, local history books, funeral records and obituaries.
Estevan City Cemetery:
http://cap.estevan.sk.ca/cemetery.records/city/index.html
http://pixel.cs.vt.edu/library/cemeteries/canada/link/estevan.txt
Forest Glen Cemetery:
http://cap.estevan.sk.ca/cemetery.records/forest.glen/index.html
Grace "Pioneer" Cemetery:
http://cap.estevan.sk.ca/cemetery.records/pioneer/index.html

Souris Valley Memorial Gardens:
http://cap.estevan.sk.ca/cemetery.records/svmg/index.html
http://pixel.cs.vt.edu/library/cemeteries/canada/link/svmg.txt

Hirsch Community Jewish Cemetery
http://cap.estevan.sk.ca/cemetery.records/hirsch/index.html
A history of the Baron de Hirsh Jewish Colony and cemetery, with an index of listed burials.

Landau – St. Joseph Cemetery
http://cap.estevan.sk.ca/cemetery.records/landau/index.html
Alphabetical list of recorded burials, with a short introduction to the parish and cemetery.

Leipzig Cemetery and Burial Information
http://www.geocities.com/Heartland/Plains/2302/cemetery.html
A partial list of burials in Leipzig and death/burial info for St. Pascal's parish 1905-1913.

Marienthal – St. Cunigundis (St. Cunigunda) Cemetery

- http://cap.estevan.sk.ca/cemetery.records/marienthal/index.htm l
- http://pixel.cs.vt.edu/library/cemeteries/canada/link/stcunigu.tx t

Alphabetical list of burials and a short introduction to this German-speaking parish.

Primate – St. Elizabeth's Catholic Cemetery
http://www.rootsweb.com/~skstjose/stelisabeths.html
An incomplete listing of interments at this cemetery.

Revenue - St. Charles Cemetery
http://www.rootsweb.com/~skstjose/stcharles.html
List of interments of early settlers.

Roche Percée Burial Records

- **Emmanuel Cemetery**: http://cap.estevan.sk.ca/cemetery.records/emmanuel/index.html
- **Forest Glen Cemetery** : http://cap.estevan.sk.ca/cemetery.records/forest.glen/index.html

Salvador – St. Henry's Catholic Cemetery
http://mars.ark.com/~rbell/html/history/st_henrys.html
Includes a map and list of burials at this cemetery, with additional notes.

Saskatoon's Cemeteries
http://www.sfn.saskatoon.sk.ca/arts/scha/index.html
Maintained by the Saskatoon Cemetery History Association, this site provides links to several cemeteries located in the city of Saskatoon, with varying information, searchable indexes or photos of each cemetery.

Saskatoon – Nutana (Pioneer Cemetery)
http://www.city.saskatoon.sk.ca/departments/public_works/cemetery/nutana/nutana1.htm
An excellent site, featuring a clickable map linking to information on individuals buried and photos of the grave markers. The burial listings are also searchable by name or burial block, with additional information on unknown gravesites and moved remains.

Saskatoon – Smithville Cemetery
http://www.sfn.saskatoon.sk.ca/arts/scha/smithvl/smthvill.html
This site provides general and historical information about this cemetery, located just outside Saskatoon, and also includes a list of burials with name, block and lot number of the grave, dates of death and burial and the individual's age.

Saskatoon – Woodlawn Cemetery
http://www.city.saskatoon.sk.ca/departments/public_works/cemetery/default.htm
This site contains general information about the cemetery and its history, a map and photographs. Also includes an alphabetical list of burials with name, date of death and burial, grave number and burial plot location.

Taylorton Cemetery
http://cap.estevan.sk.ca/cemetery.records/taylorton/index.html
Alphabetical list of burials between the years of 1903 and 1954.

Torquay Burial Records

- **Mount Green Cemetery**: http://cap.estevan.sk.ca/cemetery.records/mount.green/index.html
- **Torquay Community Cemetery**: http://cap.estevan.sk.ca/cemetery.records/torquay/index.html
  List burials for the Trinity Lutheran section and Sacred Heart Roman Catholic section.
- **Torquay Community Cemetery**: http://pixel.cs.vt.edu/library/cemeteries/canada/link/torquay.txt
  Listings for burials in this cemetery of Germans from Russia.

Tramping Lake – St. Michael's Catholic Cemetery
http://www.rootsweb.com/~skstjose/stcharles.html
A listing of burials of early settlers of this community.

<u>*Land Records*</u>

Krist School District Land Plat
http://www.rootsweb.com/~cansk/Saskatchewan/krist.htm
A map of the district in the Battleford region, showing landowners near the school circa 1908.

<u>*Data for Specific Cultural Groups*</u>

Known and Suspected Zichydorfers in the 1901 Census of Canada

- **Part 1**: http://www.feefhs.org/zva/1901cen1.html
- **Part 2**: http://www.feefhs.org/zva/1901cen2.html

Extracted records on Zichydorf emigrants to Canada, mostly in present-day Saskatchewan.

Passengers from Zichydorf Aboard the S.S. *Adria* (Hamburg to Halifax)
http://www.feefhs.org/zva/zpaslst1.html
1903 list of immigrants, most of whom continued on to Winnipeg and Regina.

Société Historique de la Saskatchewan: Banque de Données
http://www.dlcwest.com/~acfc/Associations/socihist/Banques/donnees.html
Indexes to *Histoire des Franco-Canadiens de la Saskatchewan* by Richard Lapointe and Lucille Tessier and *Les Français dans l'Ouest Canadien* by Donatien Frémont, with others to be added.

Museums/Historic Sites & Groups

Museums and Historic Sites

Batoche National Historic Site – Duck Lake, SK [English & French]
http://Parkscanada.pch.gc.ca/parks/Saskatchewan/batoche/batochee.htm
Commemorating the site of the last battle of the Saskatchewan rebellion of 1885 and the history and culture of the Métis of the region. An online tour of the historic site is available.

Biggar Museum and Gallery – Biggar, SK
http://susan.chin.gc.ca:8016/BASIS/guide/user/search/DDW?M=1&U=1&W=GUIDE_KEY=866
Exhibits and artifacts relating to settlement and local history up to 1955.

Claybank Brick Plant National Historic Site and Museum – RM of Elmsthorpe
http://www.moosejaw.net/bricks/index.html
Tour the brick making process "from clay to kiln" in this operational factory, frozen in time in the 1920's. Features 10 beehive kilns, machinery, outbuildings and the Boarding House.

Duck Lake Regional Interpretive Centre (Museum and Gallery) – Duck Lake, SK
http://susan.chin.gc.ca:8016/BASIS/guide/user/search/DDW?M=1&U=1&W=GUIDE_KEY=1224
Exhibits of artifacts relating to Indian, Métis and pioneer history in Saskatchewan. Themes include origins, religion, education, law & rebellion, economics and commerce.

Fort Battleford National Historic Site – Battleford, SK
[English & French]
http://parkscanada.pch.gc.ca/parks/saskatchewan/fort_battleford/fort_battleforde.htm
Four original buildings, a reconstructed stockade and bastion mark this Northwest Mounted Police fort, in use from 1896-1924. A history and online tour are available.

Fort Saskatchewan Museum and Historic Site – Fort Saskatchewan, SK
http://www.fortsaskinfo.com/museum/
Information on the history and development of this town, including a restored courthouse, school, church and typical home. The site also provides information on historic places and personalities from the area. Programs and event info listed.

Fort Walsh National Historic Site – near Maple Creek, SK
[English & French]
http://parkscanada.pch.gc.ca/parks/saskatchewan/fort_walsh/fort_walshe.htm
This former North West Mounted Police/Royal Canadian Mounted Police post now includes the Fort Walsh townsite, two cemeteries and a reconstructed whiskey trading post. Online tour.

Grand Coteau Heritage and Cultural Centre – Shauvanon, SK
http://susan.chin.gc.ca:8016/BASIS/guide/user/search/DDW?M=1&U=1&W=GUIDE_KEY=1075
Houses natural history, early settlement and art exhibits pertaining to the region.

Humboldt and District Museum and Gallery – Humboldt, SK
http://susan.chin.gc.ca:8016/BASIS/guide/user/search/DDW?M=1&U=1&W=GUIDE_KEY=1684
Exhibits on the human and natural history of the town – originally a German Roman Catholic settlement. Two floors of displays in the 1912 former Post Office building.

Melfort and District Museum – Melfort, SK
http://www.nlnet.melfort.sk.ca/museum/museum00.htm
A reconstructed pioneer village, including a 1907 school, pioneer general store, blacksmith shop, log home, post office and other buildings. Features displays of agricultural equipment.

Morse Museum and Cultural Centre – Morse, SK
http://susan.chin.gc.ca:8016/BASIS/guide/user/search/DDW?M=1&U=1&W=GUIDE_KEY=1622
Housed in a former 1912 school, this museum features a reconstructed classroom, and displays of reconstructed pioneer kitchen, bedroom, living room, bachelor's shack and town history.

Motherwell Homestead National Historic Site [English & French]
http://parkscanada.pch.gc.ca/parks/saskatchewan/motherwell_homestead/motherwell_homesteade.htm
A typical prairie homestead, the former home W.R. Motherwell commemorated the agriculture, lifestyle and costumes of the early 20th century with exhibits and costumed interpreters.

Regina Plains Museum – Regina, SK
http://susan.chin.gc.ca:8016/BASIS/guide/user/search/DDW?M=1&U=1&W=GUIDE_KEY=1435
Exhibits in this museum dedicated to cultural, social, political and economic history of Regina include Community of Cultures, Regina's Market Square and At Home in Regina.

Saskatchewan Western Development Museum – various locations
http://www.wdmuseum.sk.ca/index.html
The museum of social and economic history for the province of Saskatchewan. Offers many events and courses in steam engine operation, wheelwrighting and blacksmithing. Branches:

- **Moose Jaw** (History of Transportation): http://www.wdmuseum.sk.ca/mj.html
- **North Battleford** (Heritage Farm & Village): http://www.wdmuseum.sk.ca/nb.html
- **Saskatoon** (1910 Boomtown): http://www.wdmuseum.sk.ca/stoon.html
- **Yorkton** (Story of People): http://www.wdmuseum.sk.ca/yk.html

Willow Bunch Museum – Willow Bunch, SK [English & French]
http://www.quantumlynx.com/fts/musee/
Celebrating the history of the community and its prominent citizens, including many Francophone families. Extensive information online, with a virtual gallery tour.

Military, Native and Historic Groups

Tribes and Bands of Saskatchewan
http://hanksville.phast.umass.edu:8000/cultprop/contacts/tribal/SK.html
A list of the various tribal groups in the province, with contact information for each.

Provincial and Local History and Photos

Provincial and Cultural History

Un Bout d'Histoire / La Parlure Fransaskois [French only]
http://www.dlcwest.com/~lgareau/lgareau/archives/Archives.html
Archived articles on the history of francophone communities and traditions, together with articles describing the particularities of Franco-Saskatchewan speech.

Francophone Communities of Saskatchewan

- **English** :
  http://www.schoolnet.ca/collections/fransaskois/Communaute/commun.html
- **French** :
  http://www.schoolnet.ca/collections/fransaskois/Communaute/communaute.html

Brief notes on the various French-speaking communities throughout the province.

The Heart of Canada's Old Northwest
http://www.fnc.ca/tawow/articles/oldnw/heart.html
Brief overviews of the province, 1885 Rebellion and five localities.

Hutterite Place Names in North America: 87 Dariusleut Colonies (1973)
http://feefhs.org/hut/h-dplace.html
Includes many colonies in Saskatchewan, with year founded and parent colony.

Historique de la Communauté Fransaskoise [French only]
http://www.schoolnet.ca/collections/fransaskois/Historique/historique.html
Articles on Franco-Saskatchewan pioneer women and men, Métis leaders, and a brief chronology of the history and contribution of the French-speaking population in the province.

Historical Highlights of Ukranians in Saskatchewan
http://www.infoukes.com/history/saskatchewan/
A timeline of the contributions of Ukranians to the province from 1842 to 1979.

St. Joseph's Colony Information Page
http://www.rootsweb.com/~skstjose/page2.html
General information about this German-Catholic colony, and specific information on the local towns and communities that make up the colony.

Brief History of the Zichydorf Colony
http://www.feefhs.org/zva/zhistory.html
Overview of the colony founded near Regina by emigrants from a village in Austria-Hungary.

The Community of Zichydorf in Canada
http://www.feefhs.org/zva/zcregina.html
The account of one descendant's trip to the former colony near Regina, with information on its founding and history.

Local Histories and Photos

Saskatchewan Towns and Cities
http://duke.usask.ca/~lowey/Saskatchewan/cities/index.html
An alphabetical list of localities in the province, many with local histories and photos.

Govan History
http://www3.sk.sympatico.ca/parlib/govanh.html
Legends and factual accounts of the beginnings of the town of Govan, Saskatchewan.

Humboldt: History
http://cap.unb.ca/sk/humboldt/history.html
A multiple-page timeline highlighting Humboldt history from the early 1900's to today.

Humboldt – The Spirit and the Soil: Early Settlement of Humboldt, SK and Surrounding Communities
[English, some French]:
http://www.schoolnet.ca/collections/humboldt/index.html
A comprehensive site covering Early Humboldt, St. Peter's Abbey, Agriculture, Communities, selected articles from the *Humboldt Journal* and Present-Day Communities.

Leipzig, Saskatchewan
http://www.geocities.com/Heartland/Plains/2302/index.html
Information on the early settlement and pioneers, with links to further information.

Melfort: Heart of the Carrot River Valley
http://www.nlnet.melfort.sk.ca/museum/home.htm
This site provides a wealth of information on the Melfort area, including pioneers and their early businesses, early families, education, social life and the Melfort and District Museum.

City of Prince Albert: Geography and History
http://www.CityLightsNews.com/pacity01.htm
Also provides maps, photographs and the city's place in the provincial context.

"Revenue Remembers: 1905-1955"
http://mars.ark.com/~rbell/revenue/index.html
The complete text of a town history written by the people of Revenue, Saskatchewan on the occasion of the community's fiftieth anniversary.

Regina's Heritage
http://www.cityregina.com/info/heritage/index.shtml
This site, part of the City of Regina's Web site, provides links to information on the city's symbols, the Municipal Heritage Awards Program and a "brief" history of Regina, with photographs and a list of the mayors of Regina since incorporation.

Regina – The History of Regina
http://142.3.223.54/~maguirer/Regina/RHistory.html
An "unofficial" chronicle of the city from pre-Confederation through the incorporation of Saskatchewan as a province and the 20th century.

Regina – Le Réginois [French only]
http://www.gpfn.sk.ca/culture/acfc/odonymie.html
A description of the Franco-Saskatchewan flag and the francophone origins of street names and place names for the city of Regina.

Village of Salvador, Saskatchewan
http://mars.ark.com/~rbell/html/history/salvador.html
A brief narrative of the founding of this town by German Catholics.

City of Saskatoon History
http://www.city.saskatoon.sk.ca/cityhall/history/index.html
Divided into three sections: Nutana, Downtown and Riveredge. Includes photos.

Willow Bunch – History of Willow Bunch Schools
http://www.quantumlynx.com/fts/musee/promme11.htm
From the first school, through the convent to today, with photos.

City of Yorkton: History
http://www.city.yorkton.sk.ca/history.htm
A brief overview of the city's founding and development, with several photos.

Family Associations/Surnames

Province-wide and Regional Surnames

Saskatchewan Genealogical Society Genealogical Query Index
http://www.saskgenealogy.com/queries/queries.htm
Search through surname queries posted to the SGS or submit your own query.

Saskatchewan GenWeb Surname Research Interests
View a list of the surname research interests of fellow genealogists, by region.

- **Battleford Region**: http://www.rootsweb.com/~skbattle/Battleford/surnames.htm
- **Moose Jaw Region**: http://www.rootsweb.com/~skmoosej/MooseJaw/surname.html
- **Regina Region**: http://www.rootsweb.com/~skregina/Regina/surname.html
- **Sastakoon Region**: http://www.rootsweb.com/~sksaskat/Saskatoon/surnames.htm
- **Swift Current Region**: http://www.rootsweb.com/~skswiftc/SwiftCurrent/surnames.html
- **Weyburn Region**: http://www.rootsweb.com/~skweybur/Weyburn/surnames.html
- **Yorkton Region**: http://www.rootsweb.com/~skyorkto/Yorkton/surname.html

Saskatchewan GenWeb Surname Queries
View or post queries to the SK GenWeb site and regional sites by surname.

- **General**: http://cgi.rootsweb.com/surhelp-bin/surindx.pl?gc=/Canada/Saskatchewan/General
- **Battleford Region**: http://www.rootsweb.com/~skbattle/Battleford/queries.htm
- **Moose Jaw Region**: http://www.rootsweb.com/~skmoosej/MooseJaw/query.html
- **Regina Region**: http://www.rootsweb.com/~skregina/Regina/query.html
- **Saskatoon Region**: http://www.rootsweb.com/~sksaskat/Saskatoon/queries.htm
- **Swift Current Region**: http://www.rootsweb.com/~skswiftc/SwiftCurrent/queries.html
- **Weyburn Region**: http://www.rootsweb.com/~skweybur/Weyburn/query.html
- **Yorkton Region**: http://www.rootsweb.com/~skyorkto/Yorkton/queries.html

Known and Suspected Zichydorfers in Saskatchewan

- **Surnames A-K**: http://www.feefhs.org/zva/zsask-ak.html
- **Surnames L-Z**: http://www.feefhs.org/zva/zsask-lz.html

A list of the names and origins of Zichydorf colonists from Austria-Hungary in Saskatchewan.

Melfort – Early Families of the Melfort Area
http://www.nlnet.melfort.sk.ca/museum/fam00.htm
This site provides brief biographies of several families from the area, including the surnames Cameron, Aikenhead, Wood, McAusland, Rush and Irvine.

Individual Surnames and Family Associations

Campagne:
http://www.quantumlynx.com/fts/musee/promme72.htm

Chatelain:
http://www3.sk.sympatico.ca/robibn/chatelai.htm#CHATELAIN

Ell: http://mars.ark.com/~rbell/html/ellfam.htm

Légaré: http://www.quantumlynx.com/fts/musee/promme15.htm

Montgomery: http://www3.sk.sympatico.ca/monta/gene/gene.htm

Turner:
http://www.geocities.com/Athens/Forum/6500/turner.htm

Wayling: http://www.cableregina.com/users/ewayling/

Chat Rooms and Mailing Lists

CAN-Saskatchewan Mailing List (subscribe)
all: can-saskatchewan-l-request@rootsweb.com;
digest: can-saskatchewan-d-request@rootsweb.com

Saskatchewan GenWeb Surname List
http://cgi.rootsweb.com/~genbbs/genbbs.cgi/Canada/Saskatchewan/General#Subscribe
Subscribe to receive e-mail notification of every new post to the query list.

Saskatchewan Mailing List: majordomo@listserv.northwest.com
all: subscribe saskatchewan;
digest: subscribe saskatchewan-digest

Yukon

Genealogical, Historical and Cultural Societies

L'Association Franco-Yukonnaise [French only]
http://w3.franco.ca/afy/
A group dedicated to promoting francophone interests in the territory in the areas of language, school, politics, social activities and history.

Dawson City Museum and Historical Society
http://users.yknet.yk.ca/dcpages/Museum.html
Includes a reference library with 5,000 photographs and records for genealogy research.

Miles Canyon Historical Railway Society
http://www.yukonalaska.com/railway/
The MCHRS was formed to promote the construction of an historic railway in the city of Whitehorse and to preserve and present artifacts from the railway industry in the region.

Yukon & Alaska Genealogy Centre
http://yukonalaska.com/pathfinder/gen/
An online resource for several genealogical resources, many of them catalogued below.

Yukon GenWeb Project
http://www.rootsweb.com/~canyk/index.html
A collection of genealogical information for the territory, indexed in the following sections.

Archives

Archive Centers

United Church Archives Network – Alberta and Northwest Conference Archives
http://www.uccan.org/archives/alberta.htm
Holds pre-1925 records for the Methodist, Presbyterian and Congregational churches and post-1925 records for the United Church of Canada for the Yukon Territory, including the Church of the Apostles, Faro, YT and Whitehorse Church, Whitehorse, YT.

Yukon Archives
http://yukoncollege.yk.ca/archives/yukarch.html
A program of the Department of Education and the Government of Yukon, the archives contains reference and research rooms with government and corporate records, private manuscripts, photos, films, a library with over 21,000 volumes and other historic material.

Yukon Archives – University of Calgary
http://www.acs.ucalgary.ca/~tull/polar/lbcdykar.htm
This site describes the Yukon material and Arctic/circumpolar material found in the archives and lists the services, hours and contact information for the archives.

Professional Organization

Yukon Council of Archives
http://moondog.usask.ca/cca/yuk1.html
A professional organization with institutional, individual and general members seeking to promote professional archival standards and practices in the territory, provide a forum and represent territorial archive issues at the national level. The YCA sponsors professional development and training grants and publishes a newsletter.

Libraries and Research Centers

Library Web Sites for the Yukon and Northwest Territories
http://www.nlc-bnc.ca/canlib/eyunwt.htm
This site, provided by the National Library of Canada, lists links to the Web pages of public, university and government libraries in the territories.

Yukon Public Libraries
http://www.yukoncollege.yk.ca/archives/yuklibrs.html
This site provides a list of community and volunteer libraries, including a clickable map of the territory, providing links to the various libraries.

Yukon Special and Technical Libraries
http://yukia.yk.net/libraries20/index.cfm
Links to specialized libraries in the territory, including the Yukon Land Claims Secretariat Library. Individual catalogues available, or search the union catalogue of all institutions.

Birth, Marriage, Death, Census and Other Data Online

Canada Index Volume 1: The Yukon Territory
http://www.oz.net/~johnbang/genealogy/yukon.txt
Billed as "Information and lists to help with genealogical research in the Yukon Territory," this site lists information on all types of records available in the Yukon, from vital statistics to immigration records, town information and a history of the Yukon – just keep scrolling down!

Vital Statistics and Parish Data

Yukon Territory Vital Statistics
http://www.familytreemaker.com/00000165.html
The extent of records available for the territory and where to write to obtain copies.

Yukon News Obituary Surname Index
An alphabetical index of obituaries that appeared in this newspaper, with page reference.

- **1970's**: http://www.rootsweb.com/~canyk/yn1970s.html
- **1980's**: http://www.rootsweb.com/~canyk/yn1980s.html

Cemetery Data

Whitehorse – Green Mountain Cemetery Index
A two-part alphabetical index of burials prior to 1976.

- **A-K**: http://www.rootsweb.com/~canyk/greymtnak.html
- **L-Z**: http://www.rootsweb.com/~canyk/greymtnlz.html

Whitehorse – Pioneer Cemetery Index
Surname index for burials at the cemetery from 1900-1965, found in the book "Lost Graves."

- **A-D**: http://www.rootsweb.com/~canyk/lgad.html
- **E-K**: http://www.rootsweb.com/~canyk/lgek.html
- **L-Q**: http://www.rootsweb.com/~canyk/lglq.html
- **R-Z**: http://www.rootsweb.com/~canyk/lgrz.html
- Birthplace Cross-Reference: http://www.rootsweb.com/~canyk/lgbplace.html

Immigration Data and Passenger Lists

Ship Passenger Lists - 1899

- *Gleaner* (June 11 – July 16): http://yukonalaska.com/pathfinder/gen/ships/gleaner.html
- *Lully C.* (July 13 – Aug 29): http://yukonalaska.com/pathfinder/gen/ships/LullyC.html
- *Ruth* (June 13- Aug 3): http://yukonalaska.com/pathfinder/gen/ships/Ruth.html
- *Clifford Sifton* (June 12 – Aug 29): http://yukonalaska.com/pathfinder/gen/ships/Sifton.html

Canadian Border Entry Lists – Yukon Excerpts
Entries at the ports of Dawson City and Forty Mile, YT and White Pass, BC from 1908 - 1918.

- **A-D**: http://www.rootsweb.com/~canyk/cbelad.html
- **E-K**: http://www.rootsweb.com/~canyk/cbelek.html
- **L-Q**: http://www.rootsweb.com/~canyk/cbellq.html
- **R-Z**: http://www.rootsweb.com/~canyk/cbelrz.html

Klondike Pioneers from Australia
http://yukonalaska.com/pathfinder/gen/AustraliaDb.html
Edited results of searches in the Pan for Gold database dealing only with Australian natives.

Klondike Pioneers from Montana
http://yukonalaska.com/pathfinder/gen/MontanaDb.html
Edited results of searches in the Pan for Gold database dealing only with Montana natives.

Employment and Other Data

British Yukon Navigation Company Personnel Records 1903-1948
http://yukonalaska.com/pathfinder/gen/byn_employees.html
Information on company applications and employees as extracted from the Yukon archives.

Index to Proprietors and Managers of Historic Roadhouses, Saloons and Cafes
http://yukonalaska.com/pathfinder/gen/rhse_ownersAC.html
An alphabetical list of individuals' names along with the establishment and years worked.

Gold Rush Participants and Data

Alaska-Yukon Gold Rush Participants
http://www.familychronicle.com/klondike.htm
A list of over 24,000 individuals who were accounted for at the end of the Gold Rush.

American Heroes of the Klondike Gold Rush
http://yukonalaska.com/klondike/bystate.html
Short biographies of Americans who were part of the Gold Rush, listed by state of origin.

Blacks and the Gold Rush
http://www.servcom.com/akblkhist/miners.htm
An alphabetical list of names of Blacks involved in the Gold Rush. Extracted from the 1900 census, post returns & newspaper articles. Includes Alaskan and Yukon locations.

Canadian Heroes of the Klondike Gold Rush
http://yukonalaska.com/klondike/byprovince.html
Short biographies of Canadian Gold Rush legends, listed by province of origin.

Filson's Pan for Gold Database
http://www.Gold-Rush.org/ghost-07.htm
Information on individuals who were in the Yukon during the Gold Rush years. Compiled from over two dozen databases and other information sources. Fully searchable.

Museums/Historic Sites & Groups

Museums and Historic Sites

Dawson City Museum and Historical Society – Dawson City, YK
http://users.yknet.yk.ca/dcpages/Museum.html
Exhibits and artifacts recounting over 100 years of Klondike history, including costumed interpreters, audio-visual presentations and locomotives from the Klondike Mines Railway.

George Johnson Museum – Teslin, YK
http://www.yukonweb.com/community/teslin/museum/
The largest collection of Tlingit artifacts in the Yukon. Also features displays of Johnson's photographs of everyday life and traditions of the Tlingit

Keno City Mining Museum – Keno City, YK
http://susan.chin.gc.ca:8016/BASIS/guide/user/search/DDW?M=1&U=1&W=GUIDE_KEY=1142
Displays on mining, blacksmithing, small town and isolated northern lifestyles.

Klondike National Historic Sites – various locations [English & French]

- **Main Site**: http://fas.sfu.ca/parkscan/khs/
- **Dredge No. 4**: http://parkscanada.pch.gc.ca/parks/yukon/Dredge_no4/Dredge_no4e.htm
- **S.S. *Keno***: http://parkscanada.pch.gc.ca/parks/yukon/SS_keno/SS_kenoe.htm

These sites commemorate the 1896 Gold Rush and large corporate gold mining in the Klondike. Take an online guided tour and read about the history of the Gold Rush and Klondike. Also includes Dawson City's historic buildings and the Bear Creek complex.

MacBride Museum – Whitehorse, YK
http://susan.chin.gc.ca:8016/BASIS/guide/user/search/DDW?M=1&U=1&W=GUIDE_KEY=1475
Includes Sam McGee's Cabin and the 1899 Telegraph Office, plus exhibits on the history of Whitehorse, First Nations, the Northwest Mounted Police and "Rivers of Gold."

Old Log Church Museum – Whitehorse, YK
http://susan.chin.gc.ca:8016/BASIS/guide/user/search/DDW?M=1&U=1&W=GUIDE_KEY=1468
A 1900 log church housing exhibits on aboriginal people, exploration, the Gold Rush, whaling, missionaries, Alaska Highway construction, children's toys and music in the Church.

S.S. *Klondike* National Historic Site – Whitehorse, YK
http://fas.sfu.ca/parkscan/ssk/
The only sternwheeler riverboat in the Yukon open to the public. Commemorates the era of riverboat transportation and freight with over 7,000 artifacts. Includes a history of the ship.

Yukon Transportation Museum – Whitehorse, YK
http://susan.chin.gc.ca:8016/BASIS/guide/user/search/DDW?M=1&U=1&W=GUIDE_KEY=1144
Features exhibits on dog sledding, Alaska Highway construction, Gold Rush routes and trails, trade routes, the railroad and river travel. Includes the Yukon Transportation Hall of Fame.

Military, Native and Historic Groups

Constantine and Brown: First Mounties in the Yukon
- **English**: http://www.rcmp-grc.gc.ca/html/qu-c-b.htm
- **French**: http://www.rcmp-grc.gc.ca/html/quar-ar.htm

An historical account of the men who were the pioneers of the RCMP in the Yukon.

Tribes and Bands of Yukon
http://hanksville.phast.umass.edu:8000/cultprop/contacts/tribal/YK.html
Contact information for various native groups and/or links to tribal homepages.

Territorial and Local History and Photos

Territorial History

At Home in the Yukon 1898-1998
http://archives.pixelar.com
"A celebration of 100 years of life in [the] Territory" in text and photos.

Depression, Discovery and Klondicitis
http://www.Gold-Rush.org/ghost-02.htm
A history of the Yukon Territory and Gold Rush, from the early frontiersmen and miners through the discovery of gold, arrival of the Northwest Mounted Police and formation of the Territory.

My Father's Father Came Over the Chilkoot
http://www.Gold-Rush.org/ghost-06.htm
An interview with the grandchildren of Thomas Andrew Firth, a Klondike gold digger who settled in the Yukon Territory. Stories from the Gold Rush and frontier life in the territory.

Northern Roadhouses: An Introduction
http://yukonalaska.miningco.com/library/weekly/aa072597.htm
Facts, folklore and photos about these institutions that served as hotel, restaurant, store and more.

Where Ya From, Gold Digger?
http://www.Gold-Rush.org/ghost-03.htm
Stories of Klondike stampeders from North American cities, including, Calgary, Winnipeg, Edmonton, Vancouver, Toronto, Ottawa, Montréal and Halifax. Clickable map.

"Women Were Everywhere": Female Stampeders to the Klondike and Alaska
http://www.kcts.org/Columbia/womart.htm
An article on the role of women in the Gold Rush "stampedes."

Yukon & Alaska Chronology
http://yukonalaska.miningco.com/library/bldates.htm
A timeline of important events and achievements in the region from 200,000 BC to 1993.

Local History and Photos

Atlin: A Different Gold Rush
http://www.yukonweb.com/tourism/goldfields/atlinhist.html
The history of this small town and the contributions of mining and tourism to its development.

Dawson City Community Profile
http://www.yukonweb.com/community/dawson/
An overview of the city's history and a look at present-day information on Dawson City.

Histoire et Chroniques [French only]
http://w3.franco.ca/afy/histoires/histoire.htm
Articles on some of the prominent francophone people and places in the Yukon Territory, as well as everyday people, traditions and forgotten locations that are part of French Yukon.

Watson Lake – The History of Watson Lake
http://www.yukonweb.com/tourism/goldfields/watson.html
The development of this remote town, including the famous "signpost forest."

Whitehorse – History of the Whitehorse Waterfront: Excerpts
http://www.yukonweb.com/business/lost_moose/books/edge/contents.html
Sections of text and photos from a book describing the role of the waterfront in the city's history.

The Yukon/Alaska Community History Project
http://yukonalaska.com/communities/index.html
The histories of Carcross, Carmacks, Dawson City, Tagish, and Whitehorse, Yukon, with photos

Family Associations/Surnames

Fractured Veins and Broken Dreams (John Conrad)
http://yukonalaska.com/pathfinder/fv_home.html
Excerpts from the book of this title about John Conrad and his mining operations in the Yukon.

The Lundberg/Kent Genealogy Page
http://yukonalaska.com/pathfinder/gen/surnames.htm
Links to genealogical information on dozens of Yukon families related to the two in the title.

"Old-timer Ponders Paddlewheelers' Past" (Art Knutson)
http://www.yukonweb.com/community/yukon-news/1997/may2.htmld/#oldtimer
An article on Art Knutson, a former deck hand and mate on the paddlewheeler Yukon.

"Wigwam" Harry Fieck
http://www.yukonweb.com/community/yukon-news/1997/apr16.htmld/#harry
An article about this Yukon character who came to build the Alaska Highway and never left.

Yukon GenWeb Surname Queries
http://www.rootsweb.com/~canyk/qread.html
Read past queries or post your own to connect with genealogists researching the same surnames.

Chat Rooms and Mailing Lists

Northern-Canada Mailing List [Yukon and NWT]:
majordomo@listserv.northwest.com
all: subscribe northern-canada;
digest: subscribe northern-canada-digest

Yukon and Alaska History Chat Room – The Mining Company
http://yukonalaska.tqn.com/mpchat.htm